AF234587

Men-at-Arms • 569

Armies in North Russia and Siberia 1918–20

Phoebus Athanassiou • Illustrated by Adam Hook

Series editor Nick Reynolds

OSPREY PUBLISHING
Bloomsbury Publishing Plc
Kemp House, Chawley Park, Cumnor Hill, Oxford OX2 9PH, UK
Bloomsbury Publishing Ireland Limited,
29 Earlsfort Terrace, Dublin 2, D02 AY28, Ireland
Bloomsbury Publishing Inc.
1359 Broadway, 12th Floor, New York, NY 10018, USA
E-mail: info@ospreypublishing.com
www.ospreypublishing.com

OSPREY is a trademark of Osprey Publishing Ltd

First published in Great Britain in 2026

© Osprey Publishing Ltd, 2026

A catalogue record for this book is available from the British Library.

ISBN: PB 9781472873279; eBook 9781472873286;
ePDF 9781472873255; XML 9781472873262

26 27 28 29 30   10 9 8 7 6 5 4 3 2 1

Index by Mark Swift
Typeset by Lumina Datamatics Ltd.
Printed by Repro India Ltd.

Osprey Publishing supports the Woodland Trust, the UK's leading woodland
conservation charity.

To find out more about our authors and books visit **www.ospreypublishing.com**.
Here you will find extracts, author interviews, details of forthcoming events and
the option to sign up for our newsletter.

For product safety related questions contact **productsafety@bloomsbury.com**

Dedication

This book is dedicated to the memory of my maternal and paternal
grandmothers, Elena and Georgia, respectively, both of them exceptional
women and endless sources of inspiration for my own endeavours.

Acknowledgements

For their support in his research into and preparation of this book, the author is
grateful to Mr Kevin Quinn, Digital Imaging Specialist, Still Picture Branch, US
National Archives and Records Administration; Mr Cédric Lafontaine, Services
des droits d'auteur, Library and Archives of Canada; Mr Mike Grobbel, President
of the Polar Bear Memorial Association; Victor Crucirescu; and, finally, to Ms.
Andra Florian.

Author's note

All dates in this book comply with the Gregorian (Western) calendar, which is
13 days ahead of the Julian (Eastern) calendar used in Russia at the beginning
of 1918. The term 'Bolshevik' denotes Lenin's party, which was to change its
name, in early 1918, to the 'All-Russia Communist Party'. The terms 'White'
and 'White armies' denote the various anti-Bolshevik forces active in the
Russian Civil War.

Artist's note

Readers may care to note that the original paintings from which the colour
plates in this book were prepared are available for private sale. All reproduction
copyright whatsoever is retained by the publishers. All enquiries should be
addressed to:

https://adamhookillustration.com/

The publishers regret that they can enter into no correspondence upon
this matter.

Title-page photograph: a mobile US Signal Corps photographic unit, embedded
with the AEFNR, at work. On the left, sporting a peaked hat and operating a
tripod-mounted movie camera, First Lieutenant Charles I. Reid; on the right,
holding a still-photo camera, Master Signal Electrician Grier M. Shotwell. Many
of the photographs in this book are the fruit of their tireless labour. In the
background, the Archangel Michael Monastery, with its onion-shaped dome
church. (NARA)

Abbreviations used in the text

AEFNR: American Expeditionary Force, North Russia
AEFS: American Expeditionary Force, Siberia
ARC: American Red Cross
BCS: *Bataillon colonial sibérien*
Bty: battery
C-in-C: Commander in Chief
Co./Coy: company
CSEF: Canadian Siberian Expeditionary Force
CSEO: *Corpo di Spedizione italiano in Estremo Oriente*
IPF: International Police Force (Vladivostok)
KIA: killed in action
MIA: missing in action
NCO: non-commissioned Officer
NREF: North Russia Expeditionary Force
NRRF: North Russia Relief Force
POW: prisoner(s) of war
TSRR: Trans-Siberian Russian Railway

ARMIES IN NORTH RUSSIA AND SIBERIA, 1918–20

Beginning in March 1918, a polyglot Allied force intervened in two remote corners of the former Russian Empire, becoming drawn into the quagmire of the Russian Civil War. By early 1919, North Russia and Siberia hosted tens of thousands of Allied troops, predominantly Japanese, Czech, American, British, French and Italian. Soldiers from other nations, including Poles, Serbs and Latvians, were also present on the ground, even if in smaller numbers. The Allied interventions were to also translate in the provision of supplies and military equipment to the various White and other, non-Bolshevik armies. In 1919 alone Britain provided the Whites with weapons and clothing sufficient to equip a force of 200,000 men, and with some armoured vehicles, tanks and aircraft, while the US Treasury extended substantial credit to the Whites, helping to equip and supply their forces. The cost of the Allied interventions for Britain alone would eventually rise to more than £4 bn (in 1920 prices), approximately matching the amount that the Soviet Union would subsequently claim (unsuccessfully) in damages against the Allies. By late 1920, the Allied forces had been evacuated from their bridgeheads in North Russia and Siberia, and most of the White armies had been defeated, signalling the unceremonious end of the Allied interventions in North Russia and Siberia.

The truly multinational nature of the Allied interventions is reflected in this extraordinary photograph, showing a mixed detachment consisting of Czech, American, Japanese and British troops and naval personnel, as they prepare for a joint patrol in Vladivostok. To ensure law and order in the streets of Vladivostok, and to deter crime, the civilian police and the IPF relied heavily on the support and superior firepower of the Allied troops. (NARA)

BELOW LEFT
Civil unrest: this dramatic photograph, taken on 4 July 1917, shows crowds of protesters on Nevskiy Prospekt, one of Petrograd's main thoroughfares, coming under machine-gun fire from the Provisional Government's security forces. What sparked the anti-government protests captured by this photograph (known as 'the July Days') was the failure of the Kerensky Offensive, in the summer of 1917, against Austro-Hungarian and German forces in Galicia. Fearing a spreading of the disturbances to Tsarskoye Selo, where Tsar Nicholas II and his family were being held under house arrest, the Provisional Government decided to move the Romanovs to Tobolsk, a safer location, thus setting in motion a train of events that would end with the Romanovs' murder on the night of 16/17 July 1918. (Viktor Bulla/Wikimedia/Public Domain)

BELOW RIGHT
Prince Leopold of Bavaria (second from left) and his staff meet with the Russian delegation at the Brest-Litovsk railway station, ahead of the start of negotiations that resulted in the Treaty of Brest-Litovsk. In the centre, Leon Trotsky (Commissar for Foreign Affairs); on the left, Adolph Joffe and Lev Kamenev, who jointly headed the Bolshevik Government's delegation. (NARA)

The aim of this book is to recount the history of the ill-fated Allied interventions in North Russia and Siberia. The history of a contemporaneous Franco-Greek intervention in the territory of present-day Ukraine and the Crimean Peninsula was explored in an earlier Osprey title (Athanassiou 2021), to which interested readers are referred.

HISTORICAL CONTEXT

The Russian Civil War was in its second year at the start of the Allied interventions in North Russia and Siberia, leading many historians to portray it as no more than an anti-Bolshevik 'crusade'. Already during World War I, Britain and France had dispatched military missions to Russia, to assist the Imperial Russian Army in its struggle against the Central Powers. It is no coincidence that some of the most prominent members of those missions, including Général de division P.T.C.M. Janin and Major-General A.W.F. Knox, would later play a key role in the Allied interventions of 1918–20, the latter as head of the British Military Mission in Siberia.

One of the very first post-revolutionary landings of Allied forces in Russian territory – that of a Royal Marines detachment at Murmansk, on 6 March 1918 – occurred at the invitation of the local *Soviet* (workers' revolutionary council) and at the behest of Leon Trotsky, the then People's Commissar for Military Affairs, to secure the considerable stockpiles of military supplies held in Murmansk from the hands of the Central Powers. The Murmansk landing was foreshadowed by the pre-emptive stationing, in December 1917, of British and Japanese naval assets at Vladivostok, to protect the city of Vladivostok and the military supplies stored there (worth US $1 bn, in 1917 prices) against the seemingly fabricated threat of the reconstitution into a fighting force of some 800,000 German and Austro-Hungarian POWs held across camps in Eastern Siberia.

The above notwithstanding, it is unlikely that the Allied interventions would have materialized had it not been for the Treaty of Brest-Litovsk, signed on 3 March 1918, between the Bolsheviks and the Central Powers. By putting an end to military operations on the Eastern Front, the separate 'peace at any cost' (in Vladimir Lenin's words) between

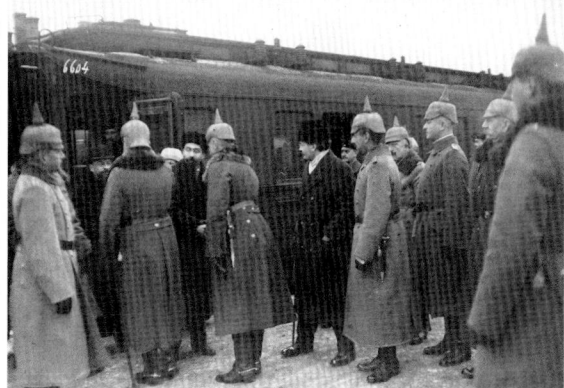

Taken in Harbin in late September 1918, this photograph captures the official Russian reception of Major-General Mutō Nobuyoshi of the Imperial Japanese Army, who has just arrived by train in Japanese-occupied Manchuria. The city of Harbin owed its creation to the coming of the Chinese Eastern Railway, the easternmost component of the TSRR, before Vladivostok. The Russian officer facing Major-General Mutō, wearing a pre-World War I uniform, is General M.M. Pleshkov, the commander-in-chief of the Manchurian Russian armies, who is turned out in a pre-1908, dark-green ceremonial uniform. The atmosphere between the two men appears to be icy. (NARA)

the Bolsheviks and the Central Powers released just short of 50 German and Austro-Hungarian divisions for service in Western Europe, at a critical point in World War I, and before the United States had brought its full force to bear for the Entente. The deployment of the bulk of the Allied troops was to continue well after the Armistice was signed on 11 November 1918 and the capitulation of the Central Powers, at a time when the latter no longer posed any threat for the Allies. By outlasting the end of World War I, the dispatch of Allied troops to North Russia and Siberia may thus be difficult to comprehend as anything other than an anti-German, turned-anti-Bolshevik enterprise.

Japan's motives for intervening in Russia's affairs (under the guise of a 'stabilization operation') were rather less ideological and more opportunist. Russia's collapse and descent into chaos following the Bolshevik revolutions presented Japan – which had already fought a victorious war against Russia in 1904–05 (see Ivanov & Jowett 2004) – with an opportunity to expand into the Russian Far East and, through it, into Manchuria and China. As of the summer of 1918, Japan supported the notoriously murderous and fiercely anti-Bolshevik (but also anti-American) Cossack atamans G.M. Semyonov, a decorated former Imperial Russian Army officer operating out of Chita, in charge of the self-styled *Osobyy Man'chzhurskiy Otryad* (OMO; 'Special Manchurian Detachment'), and I.P. Kalmykov, who was based in Khabarovsk. The dispatch of tens of thousands of Japanese troops into the Russian Far East was primarily motivated by Japan's territorial expansion ambitions, and the prospect of economic gain (Russia's Pacific coast and Manchuria were rich in natural resources, including iron ore and coal) rather than anti-Bolshevik sentiment.

Japan's geopolitical aspirations may have also been a deciding factor in the United States' involvement in Siberia, despite US President Woodrow Wilson's initial misgivings. Soviet Foreign Minister M.M. Litvinov would famously renounce, in November 1933, the Soviet Union's indemnification claims against the United States, treating the US intervention as an attempt to stymie Japanese expansion.

CHRONOLOGY

1917

7 November Break-out of Bolshevik armed insurrection (so-called 'October Revolution') in Petrograd.

22 December Start of peace talks between the Bolsheviks and the Central Powers.

1918

1 January Britain proposes the dispatch to Vladivostok of an Allied force to guard war *matériel*.

12–17 January British and Japanese naval assets moor at Vladivostok.

3 March Signature of the Treaty of Brest-Litovsk, signalling Russia's withdrawal from World War I.

6 March Royal Marines land in Murmansk with the agreement of and in coordination with local *Soviet*.

16–18 March France and Britain urge intervention in Russian Civil War.

5 April British and Japanese Marines land in Vladivostok.

14 May 'Chelyabinsk incident', pitting the Czechoslovak Legion against the Bolsheviks, marking the start of animosity between the Czechoslovak Legion and Soviet Russia.

21 May Trotsky, the People's Commissar for Military Affairs, orders the disarming and internment of the Czechoslovak Legion in Marianovka, Irkutsk, Zlatoust and Krasnoyarsk.

23 May Czechoslovak Legion commanders decide that the Legionaries will force their way through Siberia to Vladivostok.

7 June 2nd and 6th Rifle regiments of the Czechoslovak Legion occupy central Siberia and Omsk.

8 June 108 US Navy seamen from USS *Olympia* land in Murmansk and help secure it, with the agreement of the local *Soviet*.

29 June Elements of the Czechoslovak Legion, under the command of General M.K. Diterikhs, invest and occupy Vladivostok, overthrowing the local *Soviet*.

6 July US President Wilson agrees to an Allied intervention in Northern Russia.

12 July Czechoslovak Legion takes Irkutsk.

2 August 500 French troops, 100 Royal Marines and 50 US Navy seamen land in Arkhangelsk, under the command of Major-General Sir F.C. Poole, against the wishes of the Bolsheviks.

3 August Japanese and British infantry forces land in Vladivostok.

6 August A mixed Czechoslovak and White Russian force captures Kazan.

18–21 August The US Army's 27th and 31st Infantry regiments land in Vladivostok.

1 September Major General W.S. Graves, commander of US troops in Siberia, arrives at Vladivostok.

5 September The first of 3,500 US troops of the 339th Infantry Regiment land in Arkhangelsk.

10–12 September Red Army recaptures Kazan and Simbirsk.

1 October Brigadier-General W.E. Ironside arrives at Arkhangelsk and takes over from Poole as C-in-C of the North Russian Expedition.

13 October–18 November Prominent White leader Admiral A.V. Kolchak arrives at Omsk and is eventually proclaimed 'Supreme Ruler of all the Russias'.

27 November 1/9th Battalion, The Hampshire Regiment, lands in Vladivostok.

1919

16 February US President Wilson directs US War Department to initiate planning for the withdrawal of US forces from North Russia.

19 March British Cabinet ponders withdrawal of 1/9th Hampshire and 25th Battalion, The Duke of Cambridge's Own (Middlesex Regiment) from Siberia.

31 March–2 April Battle of Bolshoye Ozerki, last major engagement in North Russia. By occupying the town, the Bolsheviks succeed in cutting the Allies' line of communication to Onega.

26 April Kolchak's White forces suffer their first defeats at the hands of the Red Army.

5 June NRRF lands in Arkhangelsk, and immediately moves to Osinova, along the Dvina River.

27 June US forces begin their evacuation of Arkhangelsk.

4 July British Cabinet authorizes the Royal Navy to engage the Bolsheviks along the Baltic Sea.

20 July Brigadier-General Ironside, commander of British forces in Arkhangelsk, initiates preparations for the evacuation of his forces from Arkhangelsk, following a mutiny of local White troops and their defection to the Bolsheviks.

10 August Ironside attacks Bolshevik forces around Arkhangelsk and along the Dvina River, to ensure the safe evacuation of his forces.

27 September Last of British troops evacuate Arkhangelsk.

1920

4 January Kolchak resigns as Supreme Leader and nominates General A.I. Denikin as his successor.

15 January–7 February Bolsheviks take Kolchak prisoner in Irkutsk, and execute him by firing squad.

16 January Lifting of Allied blockade of Soviet Russia.

15 February Start of the withdrawal of the AEFS from Vladivostok.

19 February Evacuation of last British and US forces from North Russia.

21–22 February The Red Army's 154th Regiment captures Arkhangelsk.

26 March Denikin's Volunteer Army evacuates Novorossiysk.

1 April Major General Graves and the last of the AEFS evacuate Vladivostok.

31 May Arrival in London of Leonid Krasin, the first Soviet official representative.

4 August British Prime Minister Lloyd George threatens the Soviet regime with intervention in the ongoing Russo-Polish War.

2 September Evacuation of the last of the men of the Czechoslovak Legion from Vladivostok.

7–11 November Last major battle of the Russian Civil War in Perekop, Crimea, ends with victory for the Red Army.

OUTLINE OF MAIN OPERATIONS

The North Russian theatre

In North Russia, Allied forces operating under overall British command (Major-General Sir F.C. Poole, in charge of the Arkhangelsk theatre until succeeded by Brigadier-General W.E. Ironside, and Major-General Sir C.C.M. Maynard, in charge of the Murmansk theatre), saw action between September 1918 and September 1919, mostly along the Dvina River and the Arkhangelsk (Bakharitza)–Vologda–Ekaterinenburg railway line (the so-called 'Railway Front'). This theatre of operations was dominated by extensive marshlands, dense, mixed vegetation forests and brush woods, traversed by only a handful of roads, rendering the use of barges and railcars necessary for larger troop movements. Skirmishes were to break out soon after the Allied capture of the port of Arkhangelsk, on the White Sea, some 600 miles to the north of Moscow, as Allied troops fanned out along the Bakharitza–Vologda railway line and the Dvina River, and were to continue throughout the campaign. The most significant engagements took place during 11–14 November 1918 at Tulgas, on the west bank of the Northern Dvina River, at the Kurgomen–Tulgas railway line, some 200 miles to the south of Arkhangelsk, and during 31 March–2 April 1919 at Bolshoye Ozerki, just west of Obozerskaya (some 90 miles south of Arkhangelsk).

At Tulgas, an Allied force consisting of Co. B of the 339th Infantry Regiment of the American Expeditionary Force, North Russia (AEFNR), two 18-pdr guns of 67 Bty, 16th Canadian Field Artillery Brigade and A Coy of 2/10th Battalion, The Royal Scots (Lothian Regiment), came under an early-morning surprise attack by a numerically superior Bolshevik sea- and land-borne force (estimated at over 1,000 men); rumour has it that Trotsky in person supervised the attack. The two Canadian guns poured fire over open sights, for over six hours, at the Bolshevik forces. The Allies' spirited defence helped to bring about a hard-fought victory, at the price of 30 Allied KIA including 20 of 2/10th Royal Scots, and several wounded, against an estimated 350 Bolshevik dead.

The battle of Tulgas was followed by the battle (and subsequent evacuation) of Shenkursk, a small town some 235 miles south of

FAR LEFT
Co. M of the US 339th Infantry Regiment as it sets out for the front in the vicinity of Obozerskaya. This photograph was taken in September 1918, as the Allies were starting to fan out southwards from Arkhangelsk, hoping to reach Vologda and, ultimately, Moscow itself. The careful observer will detect a wagon in the distance, apparently belonging to an armoured train covering the Allied advance. (NARA)

LEFT
The Allies push south: an armoured train, carrying British, Polish and White Russian troops, pictured at Obozerskaya, on 24 September 1918. The technical device visible in the foreground is an artillery stereoscopic optical rangefinder. (NARA)

Arkhangelsk and east of the Bakharitza–Vologda railway line, on the right bank of the Vaga River (a tributary of the Dvina). During 19–25 January 1919, several thousand Bolshevik troops staged a three-pronged infantry attack, under artillery cover, against an Allied force consisting of Co. A of the AEFNR's 339th Infantry Regiment and White Russian (Cossack) troops, supported by two 18-pdrs of 68 Bty, 16th Canadian Field Artillery Brigade. This attack cut the town off and forced the greatly outnumbered Allies to retreat, under cover of darkness, 56 miles north of Shenkursk, in the direction of Arkhangelsk, in knee-deep snow and under constant fire, leaving behind large supplies of military *matériel* and provisions.

The battle of Bolshoye Ozerki was the last major engagement fought by the Allies in North Russia. Co. H and Co. M of the AEFNR's 339th Infantry Regiment and A Coy, 6th Battalion, Alexandra, Princess of Wales's Own (Yorkshire Regiment), plus one Polish company and one White Russian artillery battery, faced numerically superior Bolshevik forces consisting of three battalions of the Red Army's Moscow Regiment and at least one battalion of the 97th Saratov Regiment (both of the Bolshevik 6th Army). The engagement ended with an agonizing Allied victory, at the cost of some 75 Allied KIA against a very conservative estimate of several hundred Bolshevik dead.

On 22 September 1919, and with the Allied withdrawal already under way, a detachment of 2/10th Battalion, The Royal Scots (Lothian Regiment) was sent by river to Kandalakscha, some 150 miles south of Murmansk, on four fishing boats, to interdict sabotage operations carried out by Finnish Red troops against the local railway line. The British detachment was ambushed even before landing and suffered heavy casualties, with 13 men KIA and four wounded. One of the fatalities, who succumbed to his injuries on 26 September, was the last British serviceman to die in action in North Russia.

Conditions on the ground were gruelling, with supply shortages, constant rain (in autumn 1918 and spring 1919) and intense cold (during the winter months) making the lives of the Allied troops miserable, and their very existence precarious, even during intervals from combat operations. Pitched into an inhospitable environment, desperately outnumbered (the Allied combat troops at no time exceeded 6,000 men, when estimates of the forces fielded by the Bolsheviks ranged between

BELOW LEFT
A mixed Polish and British gun crew, operating under the command of a British Army officer (in a 'Brodie' helmet), sighting a gun mounted on an armoured train on 29 September 1918, near the US Army headquarters at Obozerskaya. The three Polish artillerymen on the right are clad in British Army service dress caps, with Polish badges, and what appear to be British Army khaki serge, single-breasted overcoats. (NARA)

BELOW RIGHT
A line-up of members of the 339th Infantry Regiment in Arkhangelsk, in September 1918. The biplane in the background is a British De Havilland DH.4 bomber, one of the eight aircraft of this type to arrive in North Russia that September. (NARA)

40,000 and 50,000) and pitted against a stubborn, tactically astute and ruthless enemy who gave no quarter and employed ruse, propaganda and infiltration to achieve his objectives, the Allied troops had to demonstrate great tenacity simply to survive. It was largely thanks to that determination that Allied casualties did not mount. During the entire campaign the AEFNR suffered a modest 146 casualties (another 65 men were lost to disease, of whom several dozen died en route to North Russia, stricken by the Spanish Flu). British and Commonwealth battle-related casualties were also relatively limited, although higher in proportion to those of the Americans. The optimism that imbued the British command in the early stages of the campaign around the possibility of the thinly stretched Allied troops reaching Vologda, to the south of Arkhangelsk, and Kotlas, further south-east, where they could make contact with their Czech and White allies before marching on Moscow, was to be proven unfounded, already in October 1918, by a combination of Bolshevik resistance, unfavourable topography and poor weather.

War fatigue among the troops (especially those from Britain and France, who had survived combat on the Western Front) and socio-political opposition to the campaign at home doomed the intervention in North Russia to failure. The intervention was marked by mutinies among the Allied troops, including the Quebec members of the 259th Battalion, Canadian Rifles, CEF, who, on 21 December 1918, refused to embark for Russia; 13th Battalion, Alexandra, Princess of Wales's Own (Yorkshire Regiment), which, on 22 February 1919, refused to proceed to the front in Murmansk; a company of France's 21ᵉ Bataillon mixte d'infanterie colonial, all veterans of the Western Front, which, on 1 March 1919, refused to relieve the Americans on the North Russian Front; and the US Army's Co. I, 339th Infantry Regiment, which, on 29 March 1919, initially refused to return to front-line duty, only to be prevailed upon by Lieutenant Colonel G.E. Stewart.

ABOVE LEFT
Standing fast: A US soldier of the 310th Engineer Regiment stands guard along the Railway Front. One can only imagine the challenges of sentry duty in an Arctic theatre of operations such as those into which the Allied troops found themselves thrust during their service in North Russia and Siberia. (NARA)

ABOVE RIGHT
Taken on 8 April 1919, this picture shows a bivouac of Co. C, 310th Engineer Regiment, braving it out in the cold. Despite being better equipped than some of their comrades in arms, with a stove to keep their tent warmer, none of the men in this photograph seem too enthusiastic about their predicament. (NARA)

The Siberian theatre

In Siberia, a nucleus of Allied troops remained in or around Vladivostok, where they guarded military supply depots and maintained order, while others fanned out in the interior of the Russian Far East. Some US troops were stationed around Khabarovsk and Spasskoe, including those elements of the 27th and 31st Infantry regiments that took up railway garrison duties along the easternmost branch of the Trans-Siberian Russian Railway (TSRR), from Vladivostok to Nikolsk, and those that were detailed with the care of beleaguered German and Austro-Hungarian POWs (a task at which the Americans excelled). The Czechoslovak Legion was also deployed along the TSRR to guard those of its stretches that were not in the hands of US, Japanese, Siberian Cossack or other White forces.

The Imperial Japanese Army and Navy aside, the most potent Allied force on the ground was the American Expeditionary Force, Siberia (AEFS). It was only rarely during the AEFS's 20-month-long Siberian campaign that its units participated in offensive operations, however, largely on account of the deliberate choice of Major General W.S. Graves, the commander of US troops in Siberia, to maintain strict neutrality – by steering clear of direct involvement in large-scale, organized fighting against the Bolsheviks – and to limit the mission of his men to guarding supply stores (such was his perception of President Wilson's written orders, at the start of the campaign). Between 24 August and 16 September 1918, the bulk of the 27th Infantry Regiment participated in only one, brief Allied offensive in the Spasskoe–Ussuri Valley region, north of Vladivostok. This offensive was conducted by a mixed Japanese and American force, drawn from the Japanese 12th Infantry Division and elements of the AEFS's 27th Infantry Regiment (nicknamed 'Wolfhounds'), respectively, under Japanese command, against a 'shadow' army of former German and Austrian POWs, reputedly 15,000–20,000 strong, that was allegedly busy laying Eastern Siberia to waste in preparation for a drive upon Vladivostok. In truth, no such POW army existed, leading the Americans to suspect a Japanese ploy to induce US involvement in large-scale military operations in Siberia.

US Army pack-mules, laden with supplies, and their handlers, march down a thoroughfare in Vladivostok, under the watchful eyes of a Russian or Czechoslovak military band (bottom left) and an honorary line-up of Japanese infantry troops and marines (right). This photograph was most likely taken at the time of the arrival of the first of the US troops in Siberia. (NARA)

French colonial troops – also known as *marsouins* ('porpoises') – in August 1918, at the time of their arrival in Vladivostok, on board the hospital ship *André Lebon*. The M1886 pith helmets and the light khaki cotton twill uniforms worn by the men testify to their provenance from France's overseas colonies across South-East Asia. The men depicted hail from Metropolitan France, as was the case with the majority of the French colonial troops deployed to Siberia. Also visible in the photograph is a Marine nationale sailor in a woollen, navy-blue uniform and a *bachi* or *bonnet de marin* (naval cap), with its distinctive red pompon; he is armed with an 8mm M1886/93 Lebel bolt-action rifle. (NARA)

In the spring of 1919, an inter-Allied agreement on guarding the TSRR resulted in the assignment of US forces to police certain sections of the railway line, separated by long distances: Vladivostok to Nikolsk-Ussuri, Ugolnaya to the Suchan River valley coal mines (the primary source of coal for all of eastern Siberia, providing the bulk of the fuel necessary for the operation of the TSRR), Spasskoe to Ussuri, and (1,700 miles further west) Verkhne-Udinsk (present-day Ulan-Ude) to Mysovaya (present-day Babushkin). Between May and August 1919, the garrisons at Ugolnaya, Ussuri, Razdolnoe, the Suchan coal mines and Shkotovo suffered considerably because of strikes, riots and constant guerrilla activity. During that period, Major General Graves's troops fought two significant engagements with the Bolsheviks, both following surprise attacks launched against them by Red Army units or partisan formations, once at Romanovka and once at Kraeffski (both in June 1919).

At Romanovka, US troops from the 31st Infantry Regiment (nicknamed 'Polar Bears') were successful, at a cost of several dozen casualties, in defending their camp against a pre-dawn all-out assault by a far superior partisan force. At Kraeffski, a platoon-size force drawn from Co. F of the 27th Infantry Regiment repelled an attack launched by a group of some 150 Bolsheviks and 35 Chinese bandits, inflicting heavy casualties on them. The AEFS's last major operation in Siberia was the Suchan River valley offensive, between July and August 1919,

The Empire of the Rising Sun on the March: Japanese marines in Vladivostok, at the start of the Allied Intervention. Japanese marines wore Western-style naval uniforms (closely modelled on those of their US counterparts), made of white cotton (during the summer) or blue wool (during winter). Their weapon was the 6.5mm Arisaka Type 38 bolt action rifle. (NARA)

Two US soldiers pose, in March 1920, before a trio of White Russian armoured cars, somewhere in Vladivostok. All three vehicles are locally manufactured Armstrong-Whitworth-Fiats, two of them (Nos 1 and 2) with twin sponsons, each housing a Vickers 7.9mm liquid-cooled machine gun. Vehicle No. 3 is the single-turret version of the Armstrong-Whitworth-Fiat. (NARA)

when five companies of the 31st Infantry Regiment launched a three-pronged sweep to clear the area of Bolshevik and partisan forces, and to reclaim control over the strategically important Suchan coal mines, some 80 miles north-east of Vladivostok. US forces were finally extracted from the Suchan coal mines and Shkotovo in August 1919, owing to the poor living conditions and constant partisan threat to their safety. Some US garrisons were to remain in their positions elsewhere on the Siberian front until 9 January 1920, when the War Department ordered the entire AEFS in Siberia to assemble at Vladivostok and travel to Manila, Philippines. Major General Graves and the last of the AEFS departed Siberia for Manila on 1 April 1920.

The limited ambition of the US forces in Siberia was reflected in the relatively low number of casualties they suffered. The AEFS's total number of disease-related casualties (135 dead) far exceeded the number of men who perished in action or of wounds sustained in action (35 KIA). It remains the case that operations on the Siberian front exacted a heavy toll on their participants, not least on account of the depravity displayed by some of the belligerents, also against POWs and civilians: the Japanese, the Bolsheviks and the Siberian Cossacks competed with one another in cruelty and sadism, with Chinese and Mongolian bandits also claiming their fair share of depredations. Relations between the US forces and their Japanese Allies were, at times, tense, with the Siberian Cossack allies of the latter repeatedly harassing isolated US troops, on occasion briefly taking them prisoner, until their Japanese protectors intervened to negotiate their release in circumstances suggesting collusion.

An armoured train in Nikolsk, Siberia, in 1919, amid several freight trains. It is fitted with what look like 4in naval guns and a Maxim Quick Firing 1-pdr (37mm) 'Pom-Pom' automatic gun, an enlarged version of the Maxim heavy machine gun, mounted on a tripod. Armoured trains were indispensable for large troop movements throughout Russia but especially in Siberia, where the road network was underdeveloped and unserviceable. (Author's Collection)

Naval and air operations

Russia's weakened position in the late stages of World War I greatly facilitated Western military interventions in its territory. Having gained access to Russian waters, the Allies used its sea ports to land troops, first in Vladivostok in April 1918, and then in Murmansk and Arkhangelsk between June and August 1918. Russian ports had previously been sealed, whether by the Russians themselves (as in the Baltic) or by their opponents (as in the case of the Black Sea, following the German-instigated Ottoman closure of the Bosphorus, early in World War I). The dispatch in November 1918 of a Royal Navy squadron to the Baltic Sea, and of a Franco-Greek infantry force to Odessa in December 1918, testify to the Allies' ability to intervene militarily in a part of a world that had been off-limits until the Bolsheviks' capitulation to the Central Powers.

Naval and shipborne forces played a key role in the Allied interventions, both in Siberia and in North Russia. The first US troops to land on North Russian soil (at the port of Murmansk), on 8 June 1918, were US Navy seamen operating out of the protected cruiser USS *Olympia* (reportedly a detachment consisting of 100 enlisted sailors and Marines plus eight officers, commanded by Lieutenant Henry F. Floyd USN, charged with maintaining order in Murmansk and protecting civilians against Bolshevik attacks). To capture Arkhangelsk, in August 1918, the Allies also relied on naval assets, in the form of the British armed yacht HMS *Salvator* (with Major-General Poole on board), the French cruiser *Amiral Aube*, with several hundred French troops on board, the British seaplane carrier HMS *Nairana* and the British steamer SS *Stephen*. Following their seaborne landing in Arkhangelsk, British and other Allied forces relied heavily on the Royal Navy's improvised 'Dvina River Flotilla', to push south along the Dvina (and its tributaries) in support of the White Russian 'Northern Regional Government', in an effort to secure the railway connection between Arkhangelsk and Moscow. To protect shipments of war *matériel* to the North Russian ports of Murmansk and Arkhangelsk, the Royal Navy also established a dedicated naval task force (the so-called 'North Russia Squadron'), commanded by Rear Admiral T.W. Kemp, whose flagship was the battleship HMS *Glory*. It was by ship that the Allied forces operating in and around Vladivostok were both delivered and, later, evacuated.

The wreck of a British biplane (most likely a Sopwith F.1 fighter and reconnaissance machine) which overshot its makeshift runway near Obozerskaya, making the acquaintance of some local trees. The Royal Air Force was deployed to assist the Allied forces in the capture of Obozerskaya, but not without some attrition, as this photograph suggests. (NARA)

In the Baltic Sea Allied forces offered significant naval and logistical support to local nationalist (Estonian and Latvian) forces. In truth, the main goal of the Allied military missions was to curb the ambitions of the *Baltische Landeswehr* and other *Freikorps* elements, following the end of World War I. The Baltic Sea was also the scene of an audacious motor-boat attack, on 17 June 1919, on the Bolshevik-seized Russian Baltic Fleet at Kronstadt, when a vessel commanded by Lieutenant A.W.S. Agar RN torpedoed and sank *Oleg*, a Russian cruiser that had earlier pounded the White Russian garrison of the nearby Krasnaya Gorka coastal artillery fortress.

Relatively little is known of the air operations, except that these were of limited scale, largely on account of the poor weather conditions and the lack of serviceable airstrips and prepared airfields in the Allied forces' areas of operation. On the North Russian Front, Allied air operations were conducted, as of September 1918, by a fleet of eight De Havilland DH.4s and, according to one source, one Sopwith F.1 Camel of the recently established Royal Air Force, which arrived in Arkhangelsk to support operations along the Dvina River. These assets were soon relocated to nearby Bakharitza, where they were complemented by a small number of Royal Aircraft Factory R.E.8s, Nieuport 17s and Sopwith 1½ Strutters discovered in crates (part of a 1917 consignment to the Imperial Russian Air Service). These aircraft were allocated to two squadrons, one of which consisted mostly of Russian personnel, both pilots and engineers, and the other of mainly Canadian pilots and engineers. In November 1918, the Allied air arm was complemented by six Sopwith F.1 Camels, which mostly flew reconnaissance and ground-attack missions, occasionally engaging in dogfights with the odd Bolshevik aircraft, operating from four campaign strips. According to one source, in April 1919 these machines were complemented by a small number of De Havilland DH.9As and six Short 184 seaplanes.

BRITISH AND CANADIAN FORCES

Composition and organization

The British and Canadian troops deployed in North Russia (the North Russia Expeditionary Force or NREF) were split between the two theatres of operations mentioned earlier: one in Arkhangelsk (the remit of 'Elope Force'), and one in Murmansk (the remit of 'Syren Force').

The Arkhangelsk theatre was the area of responsibility of 236th Infantry Brigade, originally commanded by Major-General Poole and, later, Brigadier-General Ironside. A second, brigade-sized force (237th Infantry Brigade) operated in Arkhangelsk, under the command of Brigadier-General L.W. de V. Sadleir-Jackson. His brigade consisted of 2/10th Battalion, The Royal Scots (Lothian Regiment); 52nd Battalion, The Manchester Regiment; 67 Bty and 68 Bty, 16th Canadian Field Artillery Brigade (497 all ranks); and the Slavo-British Allied Legion (SBAL), a British-trained and -commanded but locally recruited volunteer force of about 2,500 men. Many of the SBAL were unreliable elements; the members of the SBAL's 3rd Company, 1st Battalion – known as Captain Dyer's Battalion – mutinied on 7 July 1919, killing five of their British officers: Captains A.M.C. Finch and D.B. Barr, and Lieutenants T.C. Griffith, G.N. Gosling and C.F.R. Bland.

The Murmansk theatre was more thinly manned, with the troops present on the ground being drawn from 1st Company, 29th Battalion, The London Regiment; 253 Company, Machine Gun Corps; and two sections of 584 Field Company, Royal Engineers. Also present was a Military Mission, tasked with training the White Russian forces active in the area; 6th Battalion, Royal Marine Light Infantry (RMLI), which included many of the Royal Marines who had originally deployed to Murmansk at the start of the Allied intervention in North Russia (4 March 1918); and the Slavo-British Aviation Corps, a three-squadron aviation force that, at its peak, operated some 22 aircraft, mostly flown by Russian aviators including Major A.A. Kazakov, the most successful Imperial Russian Air Force pilot of World War I.

The Royal Navy contributed some 20 of its vessels, split between the two theatres, originally under the command of Rear Admiral Kemp (later, Rear Admiral J.F.E. Green), which included, apart from several capital ships, several river monitors, constituted into a 'Dvina River Flotilla' to

Undated photograph, taken at an unidentified location, showing a British Army officer inspecting what could be members of 2/10th Battalion, The Royal Scots (Lothian Regiment), following their return from a patrol. On 14 November 1918, these men – alongside a handful of American riflemen and a few Canadian field gunners – found themselves locked in a vicious and bloody firefight with a force of between 1,000 and 2,500 Bolsheviks at Tulgas, on the west bank of the Southern Dvina River. (NARA)

Undated photograph showing British or Canadian artillerymen next to what appears to be a 155mm Russian howitzer, somewhere along the Arkhangelsk–Vologda railway line. Judging by the attire of these men, and the light snowfall, this photograph was most probably taken between mid-October and mid-November 1918, before the Arctic winter set in fully. (NARA)

support land-based operations along the water masses to the south of Arkhangelsk. For its part, the Royal Air Force deployed a small number of aircraft, including fighters, bombers and seaplanes.

In April 1919, the North Russia Relief Force (NRRF), a volunteer force of about 3,500 men, was raised in England and dispatched to the North Russian Front (which it reached by boat on 5 June), to help stabilize the British positions (mainly in the Arkhangelsk theatre) and to pave the way for the gradual withdrawal of British and Canadian forces from the ground. The last of the British and Canadian forces were pulled out of North Russia by 27 September 1919.

In Siberia, a Vladivostok-based British Military Mission was established, the core of which was 1/9th Battalion, The Hampshire Regiment (deployed from Bombay, India), and 25th Battalion, The Duke of Cambridge's Own (Middlesex Regiment), composed of 800

Taken on 26 May 1919, on Troitsky Avenue, one of Arkhangelsk's main thoroughfares, this photograph documents the NRRF's arrival in North Russia. (NARA)

men reinforced by 150 soldiers of 52nd Battalion, The Manchester Regiment (deployed from Singapore and Hong Kong, respectively). While 25th Middlesex landed in Vladivostok in early August 1918 and spent the winter quartered at Omsk, 1/9th Hampshire landed in Vladivostok in January 1919 and over-wintered at Krasnoyarsk. These troops were complemented by a mixed Royal Marines and Royal Navy detachment, which manned two armed tugs along the Kama River, thousands of miles away from their mother ship, the armoured cruiser HMS *Kent*. Plans to create an Anglo-Russian brigade in Ekaterinburg, in the spring of 1919, under the auspices of 1/9th Hampshire, were scrapped following Admiral A.V. Kolchak's capture and the defeat of the Whites on the Siberian front.

The main Commonwealth contributor to the war effort on the Siberian front was Canada, which dispatched to Vladivostok a Canadian Siberian Expeditionary Force (CSEF) with an establishment of some 4,192 all ranks and commanded by Major General Sir J.H. Elmsley. The core of the CSEF was 16th Canadian Infantry Brigade, led by Brigadier General H. Bickford and composed of the 259th and 260th battalions (Canadian Rifles) – both of them conscripted units, recruited from across Canada – plus one engineer company, one machine-gun company, a North-West Mounted Police cavalry squadron, one (independent) artillery battery and various support units. The CSEF landed in Vladivostok between late October 1918 (shortly before the signature of the Armistice) and January 1919, and its men were charged, mostly, with supply train guarding duties. The CSEF began its withdrawal on 22 April 1919, with the last of its men evacuated from Siberia by 5 June.

Uniforms, weapons and equipment

The uniforms, weapons and equipment of the British Army and Canadian forces during World War I have been described in some detail in earlier Osprey publications (Chappell 2003/2005a/2005b & Chartrand 2007), which interested readers may care to consult. For representations of the uniforms worn by the British and Canadian forces deployed in North Russia and Siberia, the reader is referred to Plate A and the accompanying commentaries.

US FORCES

Composition and organization

In North Russia, the backbone of the US forces was made up of the 339th Infantry Regiment ('Detroit's Own'), which mostly consisted of men from Detroit, Michigan, and neighbouring Wisconsin. The 339th Infantry Regiment was part of the 85th Infantry Division, which sailed for England in the late summer of 1918, after its men had completed a curtailed training course at Camp Custer (Battle Creek, Michigan). Unlike the rest of the division, which was preparing to join the fight in the fields of France, the men of the 339th Infantry Regiment alongside certain support units were constituted into the AEFNR, issued Russian and British personal and support weapons and shipped to North Russia for what came to be known as the 'Polar Bear Expedition'. In early September 1918 the AEFNR reached Arkhangelsk, where it joined an international force under British command, officially on site to guard munitions but, de facto, tasked with engaging the Bolsheviks (or 'Bolos', to the US 'Doughboys'). In April 1919, the US 167th and 168th Railroad Transportation companies joined the AEFNR, and were deployed mainly in the region of Murmansk, where they offered invaluable services. Three months down the line they were evacuated to France.

The AEFNR, which bore the brunt of the fighting in North Russia, along the Dvina River and the Arkhangelsk–Vologda railway fronts, was commanded by Major G.E. Stewart, a US Army officer with cold climates experience, gained in Alaska, and decorated with the Medal of Honor for his actions in the Philippines. Stewart, who held the temporary rank of lieutenant colonel for the duration of the 339th Infantry Regiment's deployment in North Russia, was not that unit's original commander, and was somewhat unpopular with some of his troops for taking orders from the British (his subordinates deemed those orders abusive and inconsiderate, but also in breach of the US forces' limited mandate) and for being perceived by his men as distant.

In Siberia, the US forces consisted of troops from the US mainland and the Philippines Department. The nucleus of the AEFS (a force of

BELOW LEFT

A US soldier stands guard before an outpost, somewhere on the Railway Front. Unusually, the US Army equipped its troops in North Russia with US-made Mosin-Nagant bolt-action rifles, complete with bayonets and stripper clips, on the expectation that there would be a readily available supply of ammunition for them in Russia. Mosin-Nagant rifles were built to withstand the harsh winter conditions of their domestic deployment theatres, but as recalled by Second Lieutenant Harry J. Costello in his war memoirs, they were far from popular with the 'Polar Bears', largely on account of their poor accuracy, greater length and added weight compared to the .30-06 Enfield P1917 and .30-06 M1903 Springfield bolt-action rifles. (NARA)

BELOW RIGHT

A US soldier distributes rice servings to a group of interested Bolshevik POWs. The Americans excelled in their treatment of POWs, ensuring humane conditions for their detainees, both in North Russia and in Siberia. (NARA)

8,831 men at its peak) was made up of two infantry regiments, the 27th and 31st, both based in the Philippines. The 27th Infantry Regiment had been formed on 12 February 1901 at Fort McPherson, Georgia, and deployed to the Philippines, while the 31st Infantry Regiment had been formed on 13 August 1916 at Fort McKinley, Manila. Incremented by an extra 5,000 men drawn from the 8th Infantry Division at Camp Fremont, California, US troops landed in Vladivostok in late August 1918. The 31st Infantry Regiment was segmented and posted mostly along the vital 80-mile rail branch of the TSRR connecting Vladivostok to the Suchan River valley coal mines. Except during the offensive operation along the Ussuri Valley and towards Khabarovsk (between late August and early September 1918), which it joined en bloc, the 27th Infantry Regiment was also deployed piecemeal, with some of its men stationed as far off as Verkhne-Udinsk, 62 miles south-east of the Baikal Sea and no less than 1,700 miles from Vladivostok.

The AEFS, which also included several support units, operated under the command of Major General W.S. Graves, a regular US Army officer who had seen service in the Spanish–American and the Philippine wars, and was a former executive assistant to the US Army Chief of Staff, General P.C. March. For the duration of his assignment in Siberia, Graves adhered closely to US President Wilson's seven-page-long 'Aide Memoire' of 17 July 1918, outlining official US policy in Russia. Graves strived to maintain strict neutrality between the Bolsheviks and Admiral Kolchak's Whites, a stance that would cast him in an unfavourable light for the rest of his military career. Pro-Bolshevik partisans in Siberia had a tacit non-aggression pact with the US forces (unlike with the Japanese, against whom the Bolsheviks constantly fought).

ABOVE LEFT
Taken on 6 September 1918, this photograph shows US Navy seamen from USS *Olympia* – once the flagship of Commodore G. Dewey during the battle of Manila Bay in the Spanish–American War of 1898 – turned out in landing party gear, on their return from a mission inland, along the Bakharitza–Vologda railway line. The seamen are surrounded by members of the US Army's 339th Infantry Regiment and are armed with Mosin-Nagant bolt-action rifles. (NARA)

ABOVE RIGHT
Four US Marines pose for the camera, most likely in the summer of 1919, as they stand guard before a US Consulate building somewhere in Siberia. All four appear to be wearing slightly adapted surplus US Army uniforms, which give them a distinct US Army look. The US Marine Corps eagle-globe-and-anchor badge figures prominently on their campaign hats. (NARA)

US Army forces in North Russia and Siberia

American Expeditionary Force, North Russia (Colonel G.E. Stewart; 5,500 all ranks)

339th Infantry Regiment; 1st Battalion, 310th Engineer Regiment; 337th Field Hospital; 337th Ambulance Company; 167th and 168th Railroad Transportation companies

American Expeditionary Force, Siberia (Major General W.S. Graves; 8,831 all ranks)

AEFS headquarters (HQ Company; Machine Gun Company; Supply Company; Co. D, Training Battalion); 27th Infantry Regiment; 31st Infantry Regiment; 53d Telegraph Battalion; 4th Field Hospital; 17th Evacuation Hospital; 4th Ambulance Company; 7th Medical Supply Depot; 391st Bakery Company; Veterinary Field Unit

Lieutenant Colonel J. Corbley, who commanded the 1st Battalion of the 339th Infantry Regiment, pictured in Arkhangelsk in June 1919. He is turned out in the regulation uniform worn by US Army officers in the late stages of World War I. (NARA)

Uniforms, weapons and equipment

The uniforms, weapons and equipment of the US Army during World War I are described in some detail in an earlier Osprey publication (Henry 2003), which interested readers may care to consult. US Army uniform included the M1912/1917 olive-drab wool (winter) or khaki cotton (summer) single-breasted service tunic, its stand-up collar bearing two brass discs, the one on the right sporting the 'US' device and the one on the left the wearer's branch of service and formation number, and matching breeches. Olive-drab and khaki uniform items replaced those formerly in blue, webbed cotton canvas substituted black leather, while chevrons decreased in size and were inverted, to point upwards.

Officers sported British Army-style brown leather 'Sam Browne' or, in US parlance, 'Liberty' belts (but not in combat, where the M1912 web pistol belt supported the wearer's sidearm, extra ammunition and canteen), and knee-length, brown lace-up boots instead of the wool puttees and tan cowhide, ankle-high lace-up boots worn by enlisted troops and NCOs. The M1917 steel helmet was a domestically produced copy of the British Army's Mk I, shallow-dome, Brodie helmet, but made of a different steel alloy and featuring a different interior leather suspension system compared to the British original. The uniforms, personal equipment and weapons of the US forces in North Russia and Siberia are covered in more detail in Plates A and B, and their accompanying commentaries.

The standard weapon issued to US Army troops in April 1917 was the M1903 Springfield, a .30-06, five-shot, magazine-fed, Mauser-type bolt-action repeating rifle, weighing 7.6lb. Prior to that date, US factories had also produced weapons for the British, including the British P14 Enfield bolt-action rifle, which, rechambered for the .30-06 cartridge, became the M1917-pattern US Enfield, the standard rifle issued to some two-thirds of US troops during World War I. For the Russians, US factories had produced the 7.62mm M1891 Mosin-Nagant five-shot, magazine-fed bolt-action rifle, complete with its cruciform, corkscrew-type bayonet and stripper clip. After the Bolsheviks repudiated all former Imperial Russian contracts, including those with Remington Arms and New England Westinghouse to produce Mosin-Nagant rifles, the US government purchased the two companies' unsold stocks of Mosin-Nagant rifles and supplied them to its troops in North Russia.

Despite their basic sights and lower accuracy compared to Western rifle designs, Mosin-Nagant rifles were sturdy and low-maintenance weapons that enjoyed a reputation for reliability. Although the quality of manufacture of US-made Mosin-Nagant rifles was particularly high (they featured blued metal and walnut stocks), US troops never quite warmed to them. Interestingly, only the US troops in North Russia were issued Mosin-Nagant rifles: their comrades in Siberia continued to be armed with Springfields and Enfields. The men of the 339th Infantry Regiment also had to trade in their .30-06 M1917 Browning machine guns for Vickers machine guns, which placed them at a disadvantage, both because the Vickers machine gun was heavier and required a larger crew to operate and because the regiment had received no training in its handling while at Camp Custer.

A group of morose-looking, cigarette-smoking Imperial Japanese Army officers on the streets of Vladivostok during the Allied interventions. By the end of World War I, the Japanese military, which was organized along Western lines, boasting a War College, officer cadet schools and various levels of reserve formations, had substantially expanded in size in accordance with Japan's expansionist agenda and regional supremacy ambitions, boosted by its unexpected victory in the Russo-Japanese War (1904–05), and its dealings in China and Manchuria. In the background (left) is a group of Czechoslovak officers. (NARA)

JAPANESE FORCES

Composition and organization

Japan's unexpected victory over Russia in the Russo-Japanese War of 1904–05 firmly placed Japan in the league of Great Powers, enhancing the prestige of its army and navy and undermining that of its Russian foe – indeed, some historians suggest that the Russian defeat irrevocably damaged the Tsarist regime's reputation and popular support, paving the way for the social unrest that would ultimately cost Tsar Nicholas II (r. 1894–1917) his throne. The Japanese Emperor was the nominal commander-in-chief of the Japanese armed forces, with a chief-of-staff responsible for planning military operations and leading the armed forces to battle.

At the time of the start of World War I, the Japanese Regular Army was composed of 18 infantry divisions and one Imperial Guard division, backed by two levels of reserve formations. By 1915, the Japanese Regular Army had grown to a staggering 84 infantry divisions, each consisting of three regiments composed of four 600-strong battalions. There were also 26 artillery regiments, each with six four-gun batteries, and 28 cavalry regiments with four squadrons, each with 100 all ranks. The Imperial Japanese Army also fielded six heavy and three light (mountain) artillery regiments.

Born in 1856, Ōtani Kikuzō was an Imperial Japanese Army general, a veteran of the First Sino-Japanese War, the Russo-Japanese War and World War I. During the course of the Russian Civil War he commanded the Japanese Expeditionary Force in Vladivostok, at one time claiming the title of commander of the Allied Siberian Intervention. He was elevated to nobility upon his retirement in 1920 and died on 26 November 1923. He is shown here, upon his arrival in Vladivostok, on 18 August 1918, surrounded by his staff; the officer standing right behind him is possibly Lieutenant General Yuhi Mitsue, his chief of staff. (Unknown/Wikimedia/Public Domain)

Imperial Japanese Army divisions in Siberia, August 1918–October 1922*			
Division	Deployment	Division	Deployment
12th (Kokura)	11 August 1918–13 July 1919	13th (Takada)	29 September 1919–mid-May 1921
7th (Asahikawa)	22 August 1918–25 April 1919	11th (Zentsuji)	10 July 1920–8 June 1921
3rd (Nagoya)	19 September 1918–11 October 1919	15th (Toyohashi)	3 April 1921–14 September 1922
16th (Kyoto)	11 April 1919–6 April 1921	9th (Kanazawa)	11 April 1921–late September 1922
14th (Utsunomiya)	16 April 1919–1 November 1920	8th (Hirosaki)	29 December 1921–25 October 1922
5th (Hiroshima)	5 July 1919–9 September 1920	* Based upon Hara 1989	

Changes in the number of total Japanese forces deployed			
From August 1918	73,400	From September 1919	34,700
From April 1919	28,200	From December 1920	24,700

Japan took advantage of the outbreak of World War I, which it joined on the side of the Entente and against the Central Powers on 23 August 1914, to occupy all German Pacific territories north of the equator. It also set its sights on Russia's Far East territories, Sakhalin and (Chinese) Manchuria. Once an Allied intervention in Siberia had been decided, Japan contributed to it with a force of over 70,000 troops (at the peak of the Japanese intervention) or ten times larger than what was originally agreed with the Allies, dwarfing the contingents contributed by any of the other Allies. The Japanese only withdrew their military from Siberia in October 1922 and from Northern Sakhalin in 1925, long after their Western Allies had thrown in the towel on their ill-fated Russian adventure. During their intervention, Japanese troops regularly clashed with local pro-Bolshevik elements: it is estimated that, during the years of Japan's intervention, the Imperial Japanese Army suffered some 3,000 KIA.

Uniforms, weapons and equipment

The creation of modern-day Japan's armed forces dates back to the Meiji Restoration of 1868, i.e. the dissolution of the domestic feudal system and the return to imperial rule as Japan's official system of government. Imperial Japanese Army and Navy uniforms were originally modelled after those of France and, later, the United States and Imperial Germany, before evolving into more distinctively national designs.

The Russo-Japanese War (1904–05) signalled the start of the transition from the formerly dark-blue uniforms of the land forces, following the Meiji Restoration, to the more modern, yellowish-khaki-coloured military uniforms worn by their personnel until the end of World War II. The Imperial Japanese Army had first experimented with khaki-coloured fatigues around the beginning of the 20th century, issued as summer garb, instead of its former white cotton, hot-weather uniforms. The official transition was gradual, starting with the 1904-pattern (or Type 37) uniform, which was, essentially, a khaki version of the 1886-pattern (or Type 19) dark-blue uniform (but with a somewhat shorter coat), through to the 1911-pattern (or Type 45) uniform, which, subject to relatively minor modifications – such as the introduction of inserts for shoulder ranks, so that, on promotion, new rank patches would not have to be sewn on – continued in use until shortly before the outbreak of World War II. The enlisted man's Type 45 uniform (which owed its name to its official adoption on the 45th year following the Meiji Restoration) was produced

Japanese infantrymen, in a tight formation, and in full campaign gear, march along a thoroughfare in Vladivostok, around the start of the Allied Intervention in Siberia. The typical Imperial Japanese Army infantryman's uniform is on full display here: mustard-khaki drill tunic with standing collar, matching-colour breeches and peaked cap with red band, made either of cotton (for summer service) or wool (for winter service). (NARA)

in wool (for winter service) and in cotton (for summer service). Originally it sported a decorative thin red piping on the side of the coat's sleeves and along the seam of the trousers, but this was abolished in 1922 to improve the uniform's camouflage qualities. Troopers allocated to the Imperial Guard's cavalry squadrons and officers of all branches of the armed forces retained their dark-blue uniforms, for ceremonial use only, until 1939.

The standard weapon of the Imperial Japanese Army was the Arisaka Type 38 rifle, a sturdy (but long) five-shot bolt-action repeater, weighing about 9lb and chambered for the 6.5×50mmSR cartridge. Boasting good accuracy thanks to the ballistic qualities of its round and, later, pointed (spitzer) bullet and its controlled recoil, excellent sights, a corrosion-resistant bore and an effective dust cover, this reliable weapon was to remain in service with the Imperial Japanese Army until the end of World War II. The Japanese infantryman's equipment, which was practical, and compared favourably with that of his contemporary Western counterparts, included a sword-like bayonet and a waist belt with three box-shaped leather cartridge pouches (two on the front and one on the back). The uniforms, personal equipment and weapons of the Japanese forces in Siberia are covered in more detail in Plate D and its accompanying commentaries.

The Imperial Japanese Army in action, in Siberia, most likely in the autumn of 1918. Unlike the other Allied interventionist armies, including the Americans (with whom the Bolsheviks had a tacit non-aggression pact), the Japanese actively clashed with local pro-Bolshevik partisans, resulting in much blood-letting and considerable losses on both sides. (NARA)

OTHER ALLIED FORCES

French

By the end of World War I, the French Army had achieved – not without some justification – the reputation of being the strongest military in Europe, if not the world, with some 3 million men at arms serving the goals of a war machine proven on its home turf as well as on the Macedonian (Thessaloniki) front. That said, the forces deployed to the North Russian and Siberian fronts were relatively small, even compared to those committed to the Southern Russian Front, with some of the formations that the French Army fielded being understrength or recruited locally. What is also noteworthy is that, at the time of its interventions in Russia, the French Army was undergoing a rapid process of demobilization: many units had already been disbanded or amalgamated, and French troops were impatiently awaiting their release from service, factors that adversely affected unit cohesion and morale. Out of war-weariness, French units on the ground came to question the orders they received, with several cases of insubordination among the elements involved in the fighting on the North Russian Front. These culminated in the mutinies of 23 February and 1 March 1919, when troops assigned to the 21ᵉ Bataillon mixte d'infanterie coloniale (BMIC) refused to go into action. These incidents resulted in the de facto withdrawal of French units from front-line duty along the North Russian Front well before the Allies had decided to conclude their North Russian intervention. Although it appears that the war diary of the 21ᵉ BMIC has not survived, the available evidence suggests that 38 of its men perished in North Russia, of whom 31 were KIA, four succumbed to wounds sustained in combat, and three fell victim to disease.

After landing in Vladivostok on 9 August 1918, the French (composite) battalion – the Bataillon colonial sibérien (BCS) – was split into two separate manoeuvre units. The first (Capitaine Feuerstein) consisted of the 5ᵉ and 8ᵉ compagnies of the BCS, one platoon of the 11ᵉ compagnie and two machine-gun sections; the second (Capitaine Schill) consisted of the 6ᵉ and 7ᵉ compagnies of the BCS, one platoon of the 11ᵉ compagnie and two machine-gun sections. From Vladivostok, they were gradually deployed westwards along the TSRR, all the way to Chelyabinsk and the Ural Mountains, in support of Czech and Japanese units, but saw relatively little action except for the battle of Doukoskoïe. On 23 August 1918, French troops came under attack by pro-Bolshevik elements, only to be rescued by

BELOW LEFT
French troops gather at Obozerskaya, some 90 miles to the south of Arkhangelsk, on 28 September 1918, ahead of the Allied push southwards towards Vologda along the Arkhangelsk–Vologda railway line. The Allies would never make it to Vologda, which lies some 250 miles to the north of Moscow. The men portrayed are members of the 21ᵉ bataillon mixte d'infanterie coloniale, as reflected in the colonial infantry emblem (a flaming bomb superimposed on an anchor) on their Adrian helmets, despite their seemingly horizon-blue overcoats (the British troops standing at the back in one of the photographs serve as a point of colour comparison). What might appear unusual for a colonial infantry unit is that some of the men, including the bugler visible here, sport the large, dark-blue wool beret normally worn by the élite French *chasseurs alpins* (mountain troops) and the alpine infantry regiments. An entire company of skiers (2ᵉ compagnie de skieurs), apparently drawn from the 28ᵉ bataillon des chasseurs alpins, was attached to the 21ᵉ bataillon mixte d'infanterie coloniale during the latter's operations in North Russia. (NARA)

BELOW RIGHT
Four colonial infantrymen enjoy a cigarette break next to an *abri* (machine-gun emplacement), between Emtsa and Obozerskaya, 16 November 1918. Judging by the five inverted chevrons on his arm, the man appearing first from the right is a war veteran, with 2½ years of front-line service. His comrades are also likely to be experienced, battle-tested troops. Brigadier-General W.E. Ironside bemoaned the poor discipline of the French troops and their slovenliness, suggesting that they could not be prevailed upon. (NARA)

(continued on page 33)

BRITISH AND CANADIAN FORCES
1: Private, 46th Battalion, The Royal Fusiliers (City of London Regiment), Osinova, June 1919
2: Warrant officer, 67 Bty, 16th Canadian Field Artillery Brigade, North Russia, May 1919
3: Corporal, 6th Battalion, Royal Marine Light Infantry, Vladivostok, August 1918

A

US FORCES IN NORTH RUSSIA
1: Second lieutenant, 339th Infantry Regiment, Arkhangelsk, May 1919
2: Private first class, Co. M, 339th Infantry Regiment, Pinega Front, March 1919
3: Private, Co. A, 339th Infantry Regiment, Nizhni Gora, January 1919

US FORCES IN SIBERIA
1: Corporal of US Marines, Vladivostok, August 1919
2: Private, Co. F, 27th Infantry Regiment, Siberia, October 1918
3: Private first class, Co. A, 31st Infantry Regiment, Siberia, April 1919

C

JAPANESE FORCES
1: Private 1st class, 12th Infantry Division, Ussuri Valley, September 1918
2: Captain, Medical Corps, 7th Infantry Division, Manchuria, November 1918
3: Corporal, 58th Infantry Regiment, Transbaikalia, April 1920

FRENCH FORCES

1: *Capitaine*, 21ᵉ bataillon mixte d'infanterie coloniale, Arkhangelsk, August 1918
2: *Chasseur*, 2ᵉ compagnie de skieurs, 21ᵉ bataillon mixte d'infanterie coloniale, Dvina River, December 1918
3: *Capitaine*, 1ᵉʳ compagnie, 16ᵉ régiment d'infanterie coloniale, Vladivostok, August 1918

CZECHOSLOVAK AND ITALIAN FORCES
1: *Strelec*, 6th Rifle Regiment, Vladivostok, August 1920
2: *Soldato*, IV Battaglione, 67° Reggimento di fanteria, Kola, November 1918
3: *Strelec*, 1st (Jan Hus) Rifle Regiment, Penza, December 1918

F

WHITE RUSSIAN FORCES
1: *Poruchik*, 1st Light Artillery Battery, Arkhangelsk, September 1918
2: *Ryadovoy*, Izhevsk Rifle Brigade, Izhevsk People's Army, Transbaikalia,
  August 1919
3: *Yefreytor*, 1st Northern Rifle Regiment, March 1919, Dvina River Front

G

BOLSHEVIK FORCES

1: *Strelok*, 97th Saratov
Regiment, Bolshoye
Ozerki, April 1919

2: Red Army commander,
18th Infantry Division,
Tulgas, November 1918

3: Finnish Red Guard,
Kandalakscha,
October 1919

A group photograph of French Army officers, all members of the French Military Mission to Arkhangelsk, taken in North Russia, presumably in the winter of 1918/19. No two officers seem to wear quite the same uniform. The somewhat lightly clad, moustachioed officer standing in the centre of the group (wearing a fur hat but, surprisingly, no coat) is Colonel L.J.F. Donop, the most senior officer of the French Mission who, in the two months prior to the Allied landings in Arkhangelsk, played a key role in preparing the ground for the city's bloodless capture, mainly through intelligence gathering and behind-the-scenes diplomacy. (NARA)

Japanese forces, at the cost of two KIA, 19 wounded and one MIA. The bulk of the BCS crossed into Mongolia by train on 17 February 1919, reaching Harbin (present-day Heilongjiang) on 20 February. Travelling via Mukden (present-day Shenyang), the BCS finally reached Tientsin on 4 March, where it was disbanded, with its men transferred to the 16ᵉ Régiment d'infanterie coloniale save for those reassigned to the French Mission in Siberia, which remained there until its repatriation in 1921. Despite the brevity of its campaign, the BCS was cited in Army Dispatches, with several of its men decorated by the Japanese, the Czechoslovaks and the British.

The uniforms, weapons and equipment of the French Army during World War I have been described in some detail in earlier Osprey publications (notably Sumner 1995), to which interested readers are referred. French Army soldiers in North Russia and Siberia wore the same regulation M1914/15 uniforms and M1915/16 personal equipment as the Metropolitan and Colonial units of the French Army, with the addition of locally sourced cold-weather garb (see Plate E). Their standard personal weapon was the 8mm M1907/15 Berthier bolt-action rifle (or, for mounted troops and machine-gunners, the 8mm M1892 Berthier carbine).

French Army forces in North Russia and Siberia

North Russia (2,410 all ranks)

21ᵉ bataillon mixte d'infanterie coloniale (750 men), including the 2ᵉ compagnie de skieurs (232 men); a detachment of 50 skiers, coming from the 1ᵉʳ and 3ᵉ compagnies de skieurs, was despatched, by way of reinforcements, in January 1919

21ᵉ groupe de marche d'artillerie coloniale, consisting of two batteries (61 and 62) of the 2ᵉ régiment d'artillerie coloniale (total 260 men); each battery was armed with four 75mm artillery pieces

Bataillon de la Légion étrangère de Russie du Nord, attached to the 1ᵉʳ régiment étranger d'infanterie, and consisting of three companies of locally recruited legionnaires, commanded by French cadres

Elements of the 101ᵉ and 112ᵉ Régiments d'artillerie lourde, supported by three Marine nationale cruisers

Siberia (1,159 all ranks; some sources states 1,140)

The Bataillon Colonial Sibérien, consisting of the following elements:

The 1ᵉʳ compagnie (207 Metropolitan troops and 21 *tirailleurs tonkinois*) and 8ᵉ compagnie (208 Metropolitan troops and 22 *tirailleurs tonkinois*) of the 9ᵉ régiment d'infanterie coloniale (Indochina); these were redesignated the 6ᵉ and 7ᵉ compagnies, respectively, of the BCS

The 1ᵉʳ compagnie (309 Metropolitan troops and 21 *tirailleurs tonkinois*) of the 3ᵉ régiment de zouaves (Tonkin); this was redesignated the 8ᵉ compagnie of the BCS

A Serb detachment of two officers and 17 men (Shanghai)

The 1ᵉʳ compagnie (202 Metropolitan troops) and 11ᵉ compagnie (213 *tirailleurs tonkinois* and 16 Metropolitan troops) of the 16ᵉ Régiment d'infanterie coloniale (Tientsin); these were redesignated the 5ᵉ and 11ᵉ compagnies, respectively, of the BCS

Italian

Italy joined World War I on 23 May 1915, and came out of it bruised, having held off, at great cost, the Austro-Hungarian armed forces along its north-eastern border area; Italy had also participated in the operations on the Macedonian Front. Largely for reasons of military prestige, Italy dispatched to the North Russian Front the *Corpo di spedizione italiano in Murmania* (CSIM). Led by Colonnello A. Sifola, this was a force of approximately 1,345 men (of whom 45 were officers), consisting of the IV Battaglione, 67° Reggimento di fanteria (consisting of three rifle companies – 525 soldiers and 12 officers), one of the Italian Army's most prestigious infantry units; one (unidentified) mountain-artillery battery, armed with four 65mm L/17 guns; the 389[a] compagnia mitragliatrici, armed with eight 6.5mm M1914 Fiat-Revelli machine guns; the 165[a] sezione Carabinieri Reali; and an engineer detachment.

Italian forces landed in Murmansk on 2 September 1918, and were mostly based in the town of Kola (less than 10 miles to the south of Murmansk), participating in operations along the southward railway line connecting Murmansk to Kandalakscha and, further south, to Kem. On 4 May 1919 a strike force of about 220 men – *Colonna Savoia*, established on 20 September 1918 as the offensive arm of the Italian expeditionary force – moved south, in the direction of Urosozero. The Italians used this location as their jumping-off point for a successful Allied attack (with the participation of British and Serb troops) on the Bolshevik positions in and around Povienetz and Medveja Gora, on the northernmost banks of Lake Onega on 21 May. On 26 June, the Italian forces successfully defended Medveja Gora against a strong Bolshevik counter-attack, driving the attackers back at the cost of multiple casualties for the Red Army. Shortly after their successful stand, the Italian forces began their withdrawal from North Russia, a process that had been completed by 27 August 1919; the bulk of the Italian expeditionary force, including its commander, had been evacuated from Murmansk already in July. In total, Italian troops in North Russia suffered 22 casualties of whom only three were KIA, with the remainder having succumbed to disease, including en route to North Russia.

To Vladivostok, Italy dispatched the *Corpo di spedizione italiano in Estremo Oriente* (CSEO), a force of approximately 2,500 men commanded by Tenente Colonnello F. Camossi. The CSEO was based in Krasnoyarsk and Vladivostok, and was composed both of Italians from metropolitan Italy and former Austro-Hungarian Army POWs of Italian origin (mostly from the Trentino, Friuli and Veneto regions), formerly constituted, in Tientsin/Tianjin, China, into a *Legione Redenta* (the 'Redemption Legion'), under the command of the renowned Colonnello C. Manera, at the end of World War I. The CSEO had fully pulled out of Siberia, through Vladivostok, by 26 February 1920.

During the latter part of World War I, the Italian Army fielded three-battalion infantry regiments, with each battalion having three rifle companies and a total establishment of 780 men (down from the original 1,043 men at the start of World War I). Each battalion also included a machine-gun company (armed with eight M1914 Fiat-Revelli machine guns), as well as a mortar platoon and a pioneer platoon. The uniforms, weapons and equipment of the Italian Army during World War I have been described in some detail in an earlier Osprey publication (Nicolle

A formation of Italian troops (right-hand side of the photograph), clad in their distinctive *mantelli* (capes) during an award ceremony in honour of Allied officers, in Vladivostok. Next to them is a formation of, most likely, French troops. The Italians form part of the 'Legione Redenta di Siberia', a military unit of about 2,500 men established in Tientsin, China, at the end of World War I, from a nucleus of Austro-Hungarian POWs of Italian extraction (mostly hailing from Trentino and Giulia). British military intelligence reports suggest that Italian forces were viewed with the least amount of animosity by the Bolsheviks, compared to any other Allied contingent. Indeed, many of the Italian troops were suspected of ideological sympathies towards their communist foes, which may explain the Bolsheviks' disposition towards them. (NARA)

2003), to which interested readers are referred. Suffice it to note, here, that Italian Army soldiers in North Russia and Siberia wore the same regulation M1909 *grigio-verde* (grey-green) uniforms and M1891 personal equipment as the Italian troops serving in World War I's European theatres of operations (see commentary for Figure F2). Their standard personal weapon was the 6.5mm M1891 Mannlicher Carcano bolt-action rifle, or the *cavalleria* and *moschetto* versions of the 'long' Infantry rifle for mounted troops and machine-gunners, respectively.

Czechoslovak

The history of the Czechoslovak Legion – one of the most extraordinary chapters of 20th-century European military history – has been detailed in a dedicated Osprey title (Bullock 2009), to which the reader is referred. What follows is the briefest of accounts of a force that, by all accounts, had a significant role to play in the Allied interventions in the Russian Civil War.

The Czechoslovak Legion (or Corps) traces its origins to the so-called *Česká družina* ('Czech Retinue'), raised in Imperial Russia on 12 (according to other sources, 14) August 1914, from volunteers drawn from the Czech and Slovak male population of (then Russian) Volhynia. The Czech Retinue consisted of three rifle regiments, all named after key figures of the Hussite Wars (1419–34), fought between Czech Protestants and the Catholic forces of Holy Roman Emperor Sigismund, and was part of Imperial Russia's 3rd Army. Having fought with distinction during the Russian Army's Kerensky Offensive in the summer of 1917, the 1st Czechoslovak Rifle Brigade was transformed into a 'Czechoslovak Legion in Russia' on 26 September 1917. After absorbing former POWs of Czechoslovak origin, it expanded into two divisions (1st Hussite and 2nd Rifle), consisting of eight sequentially numbered rifle regiments with about 45,000 men in total. On 15 January 1918, the Czechoslovak troops were formally designated as part of the French Army, destined to join the fight against the Central Powers on the Western Front. Following the Bolshevik Revolution, on 26 March 1918 the new Soviet government sanctioned the Czechoslovak Legion's evacuation from Russia, through

Vladivostok, in breach of the earlier Treaty of Brest-Litovsk, which catered for the release of all POWs and their return home. Previously, the Czechoslovak Legion had managed to escape east from Ukraine, avoiding encirclement by the advancing German troops thanks to the heroic efforts and blood shed by the men of the 6th 'Hanácký', 7th 'Tatranský' and 4th 'Prokop Holý' (the Great) Rifle regiments.

Although they entrained for the east, the Legionaries made slow progress towards Vladivostok: this they attributed to delaying tactics on the part of the Bolsheviks, although capacity constraints were a likelier explanation. The Legion's uneasy relations with the Bolsheviks did not survive the 'Chelyabinsk incident' of 14 May 1918, when a spontaneous altercation between the eastbound men of the Legion's 6th 'Hanácký' and 3rd 'J. Zizka z Trocnova' Rifle regiments and a group of westbound Austro-Hungarian POWs deteriorated into an all-out showdown between the Red Army and the Legion. The latter took control of the TSRR, from the Volga to Vladivostok (which the Legionaries captured on 29 June 1918), collaborating with local anti-Bolshevik elements and their provisional regional governments.

By the early summer of 1918, a 3rd Division (9th to 12th Rifle regiments) was established, thanks to an influx of volunteers, bringing the Legion's manpower to an estimated 70,000 men. Following the declaration of Czechoslovakia's independence (28 October 1918) and the Armistice, the Czechoslovak Legion withdrew from the Urals and limited itself to defending stretches of the eastern TSRR against pro-Bolshevik partisans, in anticipation of their repatriation. Most Legionaries spent the winter of 1919/20 west of Lake Baikal, as the authority of Admiral Kolchak's regime was slowly eroding. Entrusted with the task of ensuring Kolchak's safe passage to the Far East (the Legion's 6th 'Hanacky' Rifle Regiment was detailed to guard his personal train), the Czechoslovaks handed him, his retinue and the State gold reserves over to the Bolsheviks near Irkutsk on 15 January 1920, under circumstances that have never been fully clarified. Having established a truce with the pursuing forces of the Bolshevik 5th Army, the Legionaries pushed on to Vladivostok, from where they had been finally evacuated by 2 September 1920. It is estimated that over 4,000 Legionaries perished in Russia.

Reflecting the origins and history of their organization, Legionaries were turned out in a variety of uniforms and personal equipment ranging from custom-made items to standard-issue Imperial Russian Army uniforms and accoutrements. Until July 1918, Czechoslovak units were mostly kitted out in former Russian Army uniforms. Men of lower ranks wore Russian *furashkas* often with purposely crumpled crowns (during the summer months) along with pocketless *gymnastiorka* tunics, breeches and infantry greatcoats, while various types of 'Frenchies' were worn by the officers, featuring four patch pockets with bow pleats, and Imperial Russian Army officers' equipment. With time, the use of custom-made items increased: the members of some Czechoslovak regiments took to wearing *calot*-type sidecaps modelled after those of the French Army, with a slanted white-and-red ribbon sewn on their front. Sleeve shields were introduced and the wearing of Imperial Russian cockades was banned; these were to be covered by a diagonal white-and-red ribbon. *Sui generis* kepi-like, square-visored hats featuring a national shield were introduced and, finally, genuinely Czechoslovak uniforms were issued, but only close to the time of the Legion's evacuation from Vladivostok (see Figure F1). In August 1919 a new-model greatcoat was also introduced, for use by all ranks, to replace the Russian Army-issue greatcoat: the new-model greatcoat was double-breasted, with two rows of five buttons, and featured straight cuffs and side welt pockets with straight flaps. One of the few Russian Army uniform items to remain in use throughout was the *papakha* (fur hat), invaluable during winter.

The weapons carried by the Legionaries were also a mix of Russian-issue items with captured Japanese, Bulgarian, German and Austro-Hungarian models, and included, for instance, M1891 Mosin-Nagant and Austro-Hungarian M1895 Mannlicher bolt-action rifles. Illustrative samples of the uniforms, personal equipment and weapons of the Czechoslovak Legionaries appear in Plate F.

RUSSIAN FORCES

Not all anti-Bolshevik forces were pro-Monarchist, and not all anti-Western partisan forces were fully aligned with the Bolshevik movement and its political agenda, which renders the drawing of a sharp distinction between Whites and Reds a rather tricky proposition. With the above consideration in mind, what follows is an attempt to provide a very rough sketch of the forces fielded by the Whites and the Bolsheviks, acknowledging from the outset the lack of reliable information on their exact numbers and disposition.

Whites

The Whites owed their name to the cream-coloured summer uniforms of the 'old' Imperial Russian Army. The natural association between that colour and the Tsarist regime did not endear the Whites to large segments of the Russian public, who correlated Imperial Russian Army uniforms, and their gold-braided *pogoni* (shoulder boards), with the injustices of the old elites, and their disastrous management of World War I. In truth, the term 'White' did not always reflect the political leanings of those who had joined their ranks, many of whom were anti-Bolshevik without necessarily being pro-Monarchist. That was certainly true of many of those recruited to fight for the Whites during the Russian Civil War, often against their will: their political persuasions varied greatly, from the pro-Monarchist

Lieutenant General Y.-L.K. Miller. Born in 1867, in Daugavpils, Latvia, to an aristocratic Baltic German family, he was an Imperial Russian Army officer and among the leaders of the White movement, both during the Russian Civil War and thereafter. During the Allied Intervention, he served as Governor-General of North Russia, based in Arkhangelsk. He is decorated with the Cross Order of St Vladimir (Military Division), III Class (with Swords), and bears what appears to be the Imperial Nicholas Military Academy graduate badge. After the end of the Russian Civil War he settled in France, where he acted, between 1930 and 1937, as chairman of the Russian All-Military Union, an anti-Bolshevik organization composed of exiled former Imperial Russian Army officers. In 1937, he was kidnapped by Soviet intelligence agents in Paris, France, and smuggled to the Soviet Union, where he was tortured and subsequently executed in Moscow, on 11 May 1939. (NARA)

to the liberal and the moderately socialist. That said, the White forces in the areas of the Allied interventions explored in this work were, by and large, led by Imperial Russian Army veterans, in their majority career officers with an anti-Bolshevik agenda. That was, for instance, true of Admiral Kolchak's 'Siberian Army', the largest White army beyond the Ural Mountains. In August 1918, when it was still a volunteer force, Kolchak's command, divided into three corps, consisted of no fewer than 23 four-regiment divisions (23,147 infantrymen, 14,888 cavalrymen and 22,224 unarmed volunteers); the 'Special Manchurian Detachment', commanded by Ataman G.M. Semyonov, a former Imperial Russian Army officer, consisting of two rifle regiments, one 'Jäger' battalion, one artillery division, two cavalry regiments and one horse-drawn artillery battalion; and the 1st Transbaikal Cossack Division, which retained the cadres of an homonymous Tsarist-era military formation. Similarly, the last and longest-serving commander-in-chief of the 'Army of the North', the main anti-Bolshevik organized military force in North Russia, was Lieutenant General Y.-L.K. Miller, Governor-General of Northern Russia, who, during World War I, had headed the Moscow military district and commanded the 5th Army.

While the Monarchist leanings of many of those who served with the White armies were reflected in their uniforms, not all White forces donned regulation Imperial Russian Army outfits: period photographs often show unkempt troops, in threadbare, non-regulation and unsoldierly uniforms. Others fared better, as in the case of the locally recruited members of the SBAL and the White Karelian forces, who were turned out in British Army surplus uniforms (adorned with local insignia) and equipment, and the men of the French-established 'Bataillon de la Légion Etrangère de Russie du Nord', who were dressed and kitted out by the French until their unit's dissolution in the late summer of 1919. By the end of the Allied interventions, the use of British clothing and boots, as well as Allied weapons and ammunition, had become commonplace among the White forces (less so among their Bolshevik foes). White troops dressed in uniform items provided by the Entente countries often displayed the rank insignia of the Imperial Russian Army (mostly in khaki). That said, uniform variations were commonplace within the White armies: for instance, whereas Semyonov's troops wore shoulder boards on their tunics, to emphasize their political affiliation and the continuity between their units and the Imperial Russian Army, the more democratically oriented Northern Region Forces and the Siberian Army had originally opted for chevron-type lace (pointing upwards or downwards, depending on rank), gold lace (for general officers) and sleeve stripes, respectively, before reverting to the use of shoulder boards, later in conflict. By contrast, although retaining the traditional symbols of the Russian Army, Semyonov's troops also sported distinctive features, such as a sleeve badge in the form of a yellow cloth shield (yellow had been the colour of the Transbaikal Cossack Army) with the letters 'OMO' embroidered on it and, according to some sources, a patch on the left sleeve of their shirts featuring a human skull and two crossbones on a yellow background, meant to intimidate the Bolsheviks (but, also, the civilian population).

The White forces in the areas of the Allied interventions were, by and large, of average to poor quality, and inferior in number, to those of the

Bolsheviks (who, throughout the Russian Civil War, enjoyed a broader recruitment base). By way of example, the Northern Region Army is thought never to have exceeded, at its peak, 25,000 men, of whom only half were front-line (combat) troops; the Siberian Army was considerably larger, but it (also) suffered from an acute shortage of experienced officers, while many of its members were forcibly conscripted and unreliable. In the areas under the control of the Whites, both in North Russia and in Siberia, able-bodied men were compulsorily drafted, with their numbers complemented by captured Bolsheviks pressed into service in exchange for their freedom. In Siberia, even before Admiral Kolchak had taken on the role of Supreme Ruler of Russia in November 1918, the old Siberian Army had organized a conscription programme, which, by October 1918, had resulted in its ranks swelling to over 10,754 officers and 173,000 men. At the peak of its power, in July 1919, the Siberian Army was divided into three armies (1st, 2nd and 3rd), of about 250,000 officers and men, jointly making up the White movement's Eastern Front (Khvostov 1997). After several defeats at the hands of the Red Army, and the capture and subsequent execution of its leader, Admiral Kolchak, on 7 February 1920, the Siberian Army gradually collapsed and disintegrated, with the last of its remaining troops withdrawing to the Transbaikal Region. In Northern Russia, the White Army had ceased to exist by February 1920.

The White forces in the areas of the Allied interventions explored in this work never won the trust and respect of the Allies, who made no secret of their criticism for their heterogeneity, unreliability, tactical dithering and less than stellar morale and discipline. White troops mutinied on several occasions: such was the case with the 1st Arkhangelsk Infantry Regiment, which mutinied on 18 December 1918, and the 5th North Russian Rifles, whose mutiny at Chinova, on 18 July 1919, spread on to Onega, resulting in its definitive loss to the enemy by 22 July. One of the fundamental reasons for the Allies' decision to withdraw their troops from North Russia and Siberia was the realization that the Whites were a spent force, which stood little to no chance of prevailing over the Bolsheviks, despite the extensive Allied support provided. To what extent some of those criticisms can be dismissed as a convenient pretext for the

ABOVE LEFT
A White Cossack has a minor wound dressed by what appears to be an ARC volunteer or a US Army medic; ARC volunteers wore military-style uniforms, making them hard to distinguish from US Army personnel. The Cossack is turned out in a traditional Caucasian kaftan coat, complete with its distinctive *gazyris* (breast cartridge pockets), and is armed with what looks like an artillery troops' M1907 *bebut kindjal*, a more modern version of the ancient Caucasian tribes' double-edged dagger. (NARA)

ABOVE RIGHT
A line-up of troops belonging to the SBAL, a British-trained and -led volunteer force the members of which (predominantly Russian) were turned out in British Army surplus uniforms and equipment. The SBAL (also known as Dyer's Battalion, after its first commander, Lieutenant R.C. Dyer, who died prematurely of pneumonia) had a poor combat record, marked by insubordination and desertion. On 7 July 1919, some of the men murdered their officers, with the entire unit then crossing over to the enemy. (NARA)

Allies' withdrawal from a costly and increasingly unpopular war is difficult to assess. Certain White (or affiliated) units did distinguish themselves; others stood out on account of their cruelty vis-à-vis belligerents and civilians alike: the reference is, among others, to the sabre-wielding units commanded by Atamans Semyonov and Kalmykov, who reached giddy heights of notoriety for the trail of blood and devastation they left behind in eastern Siberia, during their service as Japan's local anti-Bolshevik proxies.

Bolsheviks

The Bolshevik forces involved in the conflict in North Russia and Siberia either belonged to regular Red Army units (as in the case of the 6th and 7th Army units active in the Arkhangelsk and Murmansk areas, respectively) or to Red Army and pro-Bolshevik, partisan militias (as in the case of the 5th Army units and the partisans and volunteers active in eastern Siberia). Contemporary Allied intelligence suggests that the Bolshevik forces active in North Russia consisted of several regular Red Army regiments (including the 82nd, 154th, 155th, 158th, 159th, 160th–163rd, 166th and 169th Infantry regiments), supported by Latvian and Finnish troops as well as by naval forces, mostly active along the Dvina River (a force of roughly 25,000 men in total). Less is known of the order of battle of the Bolshevik forces in Siberia, where most of the fighting was tackled by irregular formations ('partisans') and armed volunteers, tasked with harassing the Allied forces deployed along the Russian Far East and, especially, the Japanese troops who made up the most active component of the Allied ground forces; for geographical reasons, the Russian Far East was among the last parts of former Imperial Russia where regular units displaced partisan formations.

The Workers' and Peasants' Red Army had seen the light of day in 1918 as a volunteer proletarian force, borne out of the irregular Red Guard units of Revolutionary pedigree. This volunteer force performed poorly

Bolshevik POWs on the North Russian Front, in an assortment of former Imperial Russian Army uniform items, including 'French'-style tunics (intended for use by Tsarist officers), M1908 overcoats and Army-issue *furashkas* and *papakhas*. By virtue of Order 929 (30 September 1918), Bolshevik troops were mandated to wear Imperial Russian Army uniforms, where available, but without insignia. Although the bearing of the men in this photograph is not overly military, Bolshevik troops proved to be hardy and determined foes, who would eventually eject the Allies from North Russia and Siberia. (NARA)

against the German Army during the 11-day war of February 1918 that forced the Bolsheviks to accept the terms of the Treaty of Brest-Litovsk, prompting Trotsky, the new People's Commissar for Military Affairs, to bring back into the fold of the fledgling Red Army (March 1918) over 8,000 former Imperial Russian Army officers (by the end of 1918, their number had increased to 30,000) as *voenspetsy* ('army specialists'), in a bid to improve the cohesion and effectiveness of the Red Army as a fighting force. Conscription was introduced in May 1918 and, by January 1920 (in the closing stages of the Allied interventions) the Red Army had grown into a fighting force of 3 million men (far superior in numbers to its White foes), operating subject to centralized command structures.

By September 1918, the Red Army had been divided into five armies, each with 11 divisions of 6–9 regiments each, allocated to three fronts (Northern, Eastern and Southern) and to the so-called Western Fortified Area. To keep the *voenspetsy* in check, to ensure their loyalty to the Bolshevik cause and to offer ideological motivation to the Red Army troops, 'commissars' were attached to every Red Army military unit down to company level. Commissars (committed ideologues who toed the party line) shadowed professional officers and were de facto involved in the taking of tactical decisions, receiving dispatches and counter-signing orders (Military Council orders were valid only if signed not only by the *voenspetsy* serving with the Councils, but also by at least one commissar). Despite the risks of the coexistence of *voenspetsy* with commissars for military efficiency and expediency (commissars could, *in extremis*, countermand orders issued by military commanders), the Red Army boasted a more unified command structure and greater unity of purpose than its fragmented White adversaries, which may help to explain its triumph over them. Another factor that was to prove central to the Red Army's eventual success was the fact that it had inherited most of the Imperial Russian Army's administrative apparatus and stocks, making it less dependent than the White armies on foreign injections of military supplies and war *matériel*.

At the beginning of the Russian Civil War, Red Army formations were turned out in much the same uniforms as the Imperial Russian Army. With time, the Red Army introduced variations, both to distinguish its troops from those of its foes, and to emphasize its ideological and political differences from them. The uniforms, personal equipment and weapons of the Red Army regulars and auxiliaries in Northern Russia are covered in more detail in Plate H, and the accompanying commentaries.

Czechoslovak Legionaries form up in Vladivostok, as they prepare for their long-awaited return home. The last of the Legionaries were shipped out of Vladivostok in April 1920, long after the end of World War I and around one year after the end of the Allied interventions. Thanks to their rich combat experience, they would form the nucleus of the officer and NCO corps of the newly created Czechoslovak Army. (Author's Collection)

CONCLUSION

The Allied interventions were bedevilled by shortages in human and material resources, exacerbated by the contrasting agendas of the participating powers. The forces that the Allies despatched to Russia were woefully insufficient to vanquish the Bolsheviks, and the *matériel* they provided to the Whites and to several other nationalist forces, although substantial, was not enough to turn the tide of the Russian Civil War. The Allied Intervention was to provoke much resentment in Russia, with the presence of 'foreign imperialists' on Russian soil providing the fledgling Soviet government with a propaganda theme that was useful in garnering political support for their cause, both at home and abroad. Soviet historiography effectively portrayed the history of the Russian Civil War as the tale of the Red Army's victorious struggle against the various 'foreign interventions' that sought to change its course. Consistent with this, Soviet sources presented the Whites and their regional, nationalist armies as little more than puppets in the hands of the counter-revolutionary, interventionist Allied powers. However self-serving a representation of the historical truth this may have been, it does shed light on the threat that the various interventions in the Russian Civil War came to pose for the Bolshevik movement. Indeed, insufficient as the troops and funds that the Allied powers committed to the Russian Civil War may have been, they did take their toll on the Red Army, while at the same time denying Soviet forces the opportunity to reclaim Finland and the Baltic countries and cancelling out the prospect of an export of Bolshevik ideology into Poland and Central Europe.

The Allied interventions had two unintended consequences, one immediate and one longer-term. The immediate one was that they created a morale-sapping climate of dependency upon outside forces, deflecting White leaders from the task of building popular support for their cause and improving on their readiness for war. In that sense, the Allied interventions may well have undermined instead of bolstering the White movement. The longer-term consequence was the deep and lasting trauma that the Allied interventions left behind them in Russia, long after those who had witnessed them were alive to tell their story. This trauma may, to some extent, explain Russian perceptions of the West, throughout the 20th century and into the 21st, as a dark and malevolent force intent on antagonizing Russia, partitioning its territory and obstructing its people from realizing their historical destiny.

FURTHER READING

Athanassiou, P. (2021). *Armies in Southern Russia 1918–19*. Men-at-Arms 540. Oxford: Osprey Publishing.

Bullock, D. (2008). *The Russian Civil War 1918–1922*. Essential Histories 69. Oxford: Osprey Publishing.

Bullock, D. (2009). *The Czech Legion 1914–20*. Men-at-Arms 447. Oxford: Osprey Publishing.

Chappell, M. (2003). *The British Army in World War I (1): The Western Front 1914–16*. Men-at-Arms 391. Oxford: Osprey Publishing.

Chappell, M. (2005a). *The British Army in World War I (2): The Western Front 1916–18*. Men-at-Arms 402. Oxford: Osprey Publishing.

Chappell, M. (2005b). *The British Army in World War I (3): The Eastern Fronts*. Men-at-Arms 406. Oxford: Osprey Publishing.

Chartrand, R. (2007). *The Canadian Corps in World War I*. Men-at-Arms 439. Oxford: Osprey Publishing.

Costello, H.J. (1920). *Why did we go to Russia?* Reprint from the Collection of the University of Michigan Library.

Deryabin, A. (1998). *Voicka Interventov Grazhdanskaya Voina v Rassii 1917–1922* (Interventionist Armies of the Russian Civil War 1917–1922). Moscow: AST Publishers.

Deryabin, A. (2002). *Belaya Armiya na cebere Rassii 1918–1920* (White Army in Northern Russia 1918–1920). Moscow: TM Publications.

Hara Teruyuki (1989). *Japan's Siberia Expedition: Revolution and Intervention, 1917–1922*. Tokyo: Chikuma shobo.

Henry, M. (2003). *The US Army of World War I*. Men-at-Arms 386. Oxford: Osprey Publishing.

Höhne, R. (2021). 'Success and Failure of the British North Russia Intervention', Society for Army Historical Research. Available at https://www.sahr.org.uk/docs/hohne-hagen-british-north-russia-intervention-sahrs1084.pdf

Hosoya Chihiro (1958). 'Origin of the Siberian Intervention, 1917–1918', *Annals of the Hitotsubashi Academy* 9.1 91–108.

House, J.M. (2016). *Wolfhounds and Polar Bears – The American Expeditionary Force in Siberia, 1918–1920*. Tuscaloosa, AL: University of Alabama Press.

Isitt, B. (2010). *From Victoria to Vladivostok: Canada's Siberian Expedition, 1917–19*. Vancouver, BC: University of British Columbia Press.

Ivanov, A. & Jowett, P. (2004). *The Russo-Japanese War 1904–05*. Men-at-Arms 414. Oxford: Osprey Publishing.

Kettle, M. (1992). *Churchill, and the Archangel Fiasco*. London & New York, NY: Routledge.

Khvostov, M. (1997). *The Russian Civil War (2): White Armies*. Men-at-Arms 305. Oxford: Osprey Publishing.

Long, J.W. (1982). 'American Intervention in Russia: The North Russian Expedition, 1918–19', *Diplomatic History* 6.1: 45–67.

Moffat, I.C.D. (2015). *The Allied Intervention in Russia, 1918–1920 – The Diplomacy of Chaos*. London: Palgrave Macmillan.

Mollo, A. & Turner, P. (1987). *Army Uniforms of World War I*. London: Blandford.

Montandon, G. (1923). *Deux Ans Chez Koltchak et les Bolchéviques pour la Croix-Rouge de Génève*. Paris: F. Alcan.

Moore, P. (2002). *Stamping Out the Virus: Allied Intervention in the Russian Civil War*. Atglen, PA: Schiffer.

Nelson, J.C. (2019). *The Polar Bear Expedition*. New York, NY: Harper Collins.

Nicolle, D. (2003). *The Italian Army of World War I*. Men-at-Arms 387. Oxford: Osprey Publishing.

Reid, A. (2023). *A Nasty Little War: The West's Fight to Reverse the Russian Revolution*. London: John Murray Press.

Rothstein, A. (1980). *The Soldiers' Strikes of 1919*. London & Basingstoke: Macmillan Press.

Silverlight, J. (1970). *The Victors' Dilemma: Allied Intervention in the Russian Civil War*. New York, NY: Weybright & Talley.

Sumner, I. (1995). *The French Army 1914–18*. Men-at-Arms 286. London: Osprey Publishing.

Swettenham, J.A. (1967). *Allied Intervention in Russia 1918–1919, and the Part Played by Canada*. London & New York, NY: Routledge.

Vagnini, A. (2015). 'Il Corpo di Spedizione Italiano in Murmania (1918–1919)', in Giordano Altarozzi, ed., *Proceedings of the 'European Integration – Between Tradition and Modernity' Congress*, vol. 6. Tîrgu-Mureş: Editura Universităţii 'Petru Maior'.

Vaudable, H. (1990). 'L'intervention alliée en Russie du Nord', available at: https://www.pourceuxde14-regimentschalonsursaone.fr/_images_site/49.pdf (accessed 21 October 2025)

Wieloch, R. (2019). *Churchill's Abandoned Prisoners: The British Soldiers Deceived in the Russian Civil War*. Oxford: Casemate.

Wright, D. (2017). *Churchill's Secret War with Lenin: British and Commonwealth Military Intervention in the Russian Civil War, 1918–20*. Solihull: Helion & Co.

PLATE COMMENTARIES

A: BRITISH AND CANADIAN FORCES

A1: Private, 46th Battalion, The Royal Fusiliers (City of London Regiment), Osinova, June 1919

The infantryman portrayed here wears the British Army's khaki serge wool uniform first introduced in 1902. This consisted of a loose-fitting Service Dress jacket with five brass buttons, a stand-and-fall collar and shoulder patches to compensate for the wear occasioned by the rifle butt and the weight of the webbing, and matching-material narrow-leg trousers, typically worn with puttees. The British Army was the first European army to replace its leather belts and pouches with webbing, made of durable woven cotton material, originally produced in the United States by the Mills Equipment Co. The Pattern 1908 webbing equipment consisted of a wide belt, five left and five right ammunition pouches (holding a total of 150 rounds), left and right braces, a bayonet frog and attachment for the entrenching tool helve, an entrenching tool head, a water bottle in its carrier, a small haversack for personal items and daily rations (while in the field), a large pack, destined to hold its bearer's greatcoat or

43

a blanket, and a mess tin worn attached to the pack. He is armed with a Short Magazine Lee-Enfield ten-round, magazine-fed, bolt action repeating rifle, which, in competent hands, could fire some 15 aimed shots per minute, a rate of fire superior to that of any other infantry rifle of its time.

A2: Warrant officer, 67 Bty, 16th Canadian Field Artillery Brigade, North Russia, May 1919

The Canadians distinguished themselves in North Russia, with some 20 of them receiving Russian decorations for bravery. The uniforms worn by Canadian troops ('Canucks') were very similar to those of their British counterparts, save for their cap badges, 'CANADA' buttons and shoulder bars, and collar badges; very few British units wore collar badges at that time. The Canadian artillery NCO portrayed here wears a tailored example of the British Pattern 1918 five-button khaki serge wool Service Dress jacket (the Canadian Pattern 1907 Service Dress jacket featured seven buttons and a stiffer collar, and was deemed too tight for field service) with matching trousers. His jacket features a stand-and-fall collar, with maple-leaf brass collar badges, two box-pleated breast pockets with straight-cut flaps secured by buttons, two hip pockets with flaps and buttons, and brass 'CANADA' buttons and shoulder bars to each epaulette. His two decoration ribbons are, from left to right, the British War Medal and the Inter-Allied Victory Medal. The brass World War I artillery badge could appear on the upper parts of his jacket's sleeves, while a single brass wound stripe badge is on the forearm of his left sleeve, distinguishing its bearer as an experienced soldier. His rank is denoted by two Coat of Arms padded patches, on each of the jacket's lower sleeves. His matching-material M1902 other ranks artillery peaked cap features the Canadian artillery brass badge.

A3: Corporal, 6th Battalion, Royal Marine Light Infantry, Vladivostok, August 1918

A Royal Marine NCO as he would have appeared in Vladivostok, at the time of the Allied intervention in Siberia. He wears the RMLI's dark-blue tunic and matching trousers,

Born in 1869, Sir Frederick Cuthbert Poole was a veteran of the Second Anglo-Boer War (1899–1902) and several other African campaigns. He retired from the British Army in 1914 but was recalled to active service following the outbreak of World War I. Promoted to temporary major-general in 1917, he commanded the Allied troops in Arkhangelsk between August and October 1918. He retired in 1920, with the honorary rank of major-general. (NARA)

a uniform retained by shipboard Royal Marines until replaced by the Army's khaki serge wool uniform in the early 1920s. His characteristic peakless Brodrick cap (named after William St John Fremantle Brodrick, Secretary of State for War 1900–03), previously used also by the Army, and replaced, in the early 1920s, by a Royal Marine-specific peaked cap, features a red diamond-shaped backing to the Royal Marines globe-and-laurel-wreath badge, without the white cloth cover (normally in use during the summer months). His rank is denoted by two red chevrons worn point downwards on his right sleeve, while the single inverted chevron on his left cuff is a good-conduct stripe (the crossed rifles patch above it is a marksman patch). His weapon is a .303 Lee-Metford Mk I bolt action, magazine-fed rifle that entered service with the British Army in 1888, for which he carries spare ammunition in his Pattern 1908 webbing. By the end of World War I, most Lee-Metfords had been converted to Lee-Enfield rifling.

B: US FORCES IN NORTH RUSSIA

B1: Second lieutenant, 339th Infantry Regiment, Arkhangelsk, May 1919

A junior US Army infantry officer (for his rank, see the single bronze bar on each of his shoulder straps), halfway through the Allied intervention in North Russia. He is turned out in the standard US Army officers' attire at the time of the closing stages of World War I, consisting of an M1917 single-breasted khaki tunic, fastened with five bronzed stars, matching breeches, light brown leather riding boots and a Sam Browne-type waist belt, with its shoulder strap running over the left shoulder; a leather holster for a service revolver or pistol could be suspended from the waist belt. His headdress is the M1910 peaked service cap, which featured a light khaki-coloured mohair band, a light brown peak and an American eagle bronzed badge. The golden thread single chevron sewn on to his lower left sleeve denotes six months of overseas service.

B2: Private first class, Co. M, 339th Infantry Regiment, Pinega Front, March 1919

The private portrayed here, in the run-up to the fighting around Obozerskaya, wears the M1912 woollen khaki-olive tunic and matching legwear; a US-made leather jerkin; a pistol belt with an M1911 holster, a dual magazine pouch and a medical kit suspended from it; puttees with ankle-length laced boots; cold-weather shooting gloves; and a privately acquired fur cap. Although practical, this attire was hardly adequate for the winter weather conditions along the Pinega Front, and would only have been worn in the heated blockhouses and outposts that dotted the Railway Front, to the west of the Dvina River. He is armed with a .45 M1911 Colt automatic pistol.

B3: Private, Co. A, 339th Infantry Regiment, Nizhni Gora, January 1919

The 'Doughboy' shown here, on patrol duty, is turned out in cold-weather attire, consisting of a wool-lined canvas greatcoat, corduroy-lined rabbit-fur gauntlets and a fur cap with folding flaps. He wears his M1910 combat equipment web belt over his greatcoat, and he is armed with a US-made M1891 Mosin-Nagant rifle, the standard weapon of US infantrymen in North Russia throughout the Allied Intervention, with its trademark cruciform bayonet fixed on its muzzle.

C: US FORCES IN SIBERIA

C1: Corporal of US Marines, Vladivostok, August 1919

A US Marine corporal on consulate sentry duty in Vladivostok, in the second summer of the US intervention in Siberia.

He wears the US Marine Corps lighter (tropical) uniform, made of beige cotton (the winter uniform was made of wool dyed in 'forest green', a uniform colour specific to the US Marine Corps); a 'Montana' round hat (termed the 'lemon squeezer', due to the crown's shape) made of rabbit-skin felt, complete with a grosgrain ribbon band and a leather chinstrap; the US Marines' version of the M1910 combat equipment web belt, featuring the US Marine Corps eagle-globe-and-anchor emblem on its snap fasteners (often stamped 'USMC'); and canvas gaiters. He is armed with an M1903 Springfield rifle and carries its M1905 bayonet in a canvas-and-leather scabbard.

C2: Private, Co. F, 27th Infantry Regiment, Siberia, October 1918

This soldier on railway sentry duty is turned out in much the same uniform as Figure C3, except that he is armed with an M1903 Springfield rifle, and wears the practical M1910 combat equipment web belt, to hold his .30-06 Springfield rifle rounds and his canteen. The hard-wearing canvas web belt featured ten ammunition pouches, closing with snap fasteners that bore, in relief, the US coat of arms; distinct pistol and revolver cartridge versions also existed.

C3: Private first class, Co. A, 31st Infantry Regiment, Siberia, April 1919

A 'Polar Bear' in Siberia (the divisional patch on his upper left sleeve features the letter 'S' (for Siberia) superimposed on the silhouette of a standing bear). He wears the M1912 woollen khaki-olive tunic, matching legwear, a British-supplied leather jerkin, khaki puttees, natural-coloured leather ankle boots and the M1917 helmet (the sandy-green, manganese-steel US version of the British Brodie helmet). His single-breasted tunic features a standing collar fastened with five bronze buttons (these were adorned with the US coat of arms, in the form of an eagle device), and its collar bears two bronze discs on each side; the left one indicated the wearer's branch of service and the right one the initials 'US', for regular infantry units. He is armed with a BAR light machine gun and a holstered M1911 Browning pistol, and carries spare ammunition for his weapon in an M1918 BAR webbing magazine cartridge belt.

D: JAPANESE FORCES

D1: Private 1st class, 12th Infantry Division, Ussuri Valley, September 1918

A Japanese infantryman in marching order, as he would have appeared at the time of the short-lived joint Japanese–US campaign along the Ussuri Valley. His summer Type 45 uniform, adopted in 1913, consists of a single-breasted mustard coat with false cuffs closing with five brass buttons, and matching-colour trousers constrained by puttees. The coat features a standing ('China') collar fastened with a hook; swallow-tail-ended collar tabs in the colour of the infantry (red); a metal number clip attached on the collar tabs, to display the wearer's regimental number; vertical shoulder rank *passants*; and two breast pockets (officers' coats had four pockets, including two on the coat's skirts). His headdress is the Imperial Japanese Army's flat-topped, peaked service cap featuring a peripheral, coloured band with a five-pointed bronze star cockade, and red piping along its crown.

D2: Captain, Medical Corps, 7th Infantry Division, Manchuria, November 1918

This plate, which is based on a period photograph, depicts a captain of the Medical Corps (note the dark-green facings on his tunic's standing collar), in standard service uniform and

Taken on 28 June 1919, around the time of the evacuation from North Russia of the 1st Battalion, 310th Engineer Regiment, this photograph, shot in Solombala, a suburb of Arkhangelsk, shows the battalion colours being carried by Colour Sergeant W.M. Monroe. The colour guards, Privates B.H. Layton (at left) and G.W. Bailey (at right), are the only Native Americans known to have served in North Russia during the Allied Intervention. (NARA)

felt boots. As with all Japanese military officers, he wears a sword, a distinction of rank but also a tool of his trade; swords were used in combat, mostly to direct troops, as well as for rituals. His is the Type 32 military sword, introduced in 1899 for use in the Army and the Navy alike (although the naval version's grip backplate was slimmer). This was an interesting hybrid, combining the exterior appearance of a Western sabre with a traditional *katana*-like blade. Called *Kyu-Gunto* or 'old military sword', this sturdy weapon was in production between 1875 and 1934. There was also an NCO version of the *Kyu-Gunto*, which was simpler in design and less embellished, although both versions were mass-produced, industrial products. His decoration is the Order of the Sacred Treasure (*Zuihosho*), established in January 1888, and awarded to military (but also civilian) personnel who had distinguished themselves through long and meritorious service.

D3: Corporal, 58th Infantry Regiment, Transbaikalia, April 1920

A Japanese NCO in winter order. His outfit and equipment are the same as those of Figure D1, except for his single-breasted woollen winter greatcoat, which is adorned with the same, French-style, vertical shoulder rank *passants* (patches) as his tunic. A double-breasted, fur-lined, quilted greatcoat also existed, which featured fur-trimmed cuffs and collar. The Imperial Japanese Army had not issued cold-weather headgear to its men, nor did it provide them with protective helmets until the 1930s: until then, its men went into combat with their standard-issue visored caps as their only head protection, against snow or shrapnel. He is armed with a 6.5mm Type 30 Arisaka box-fed, bolt-action rifle, with its sword-like bayonet attached to its muzzle.

E: FRENCH FORCES

E1: *Capitaine*, 21ᵉ bataillon mixte d'infanterie coloniale, Arkhangelsk, August 1918

The uniforms of the French Army underwent drastic changes since the start of World War I, from the colourful outfits of August 1914 to the more practical horizon-blue uniforms worn by the time of the Armistice. The officer depicted here wears the post-1915 wool uniform, consisting of a tunic with a stand-and-fall collar, two pleated patch breast pockets and two larger pleated skirt pockets (the former with pointed and the latter with straight buttoned flaps), and a single pleat in the skirt's rear; matching-colour 'semi-breeches' reaching below the knee; and part-laced, tan leather boots. His rank is displayed by way of three golden lace straight bars, measuring 12mm by 35mm, sewn in above the lower cuffs of his tunic's sleeves. The five golden lace inverted service chevrons on the wearer's upper left arm indicate three full years of front-line service (*chevrons de présence aux armées* or *brisques d'ancienneté*), making the captain depicted here a *briscard* (war veteran). The three similar-styled chevrons appearing on the upper right arm denote three separate war wounds. He is equipped with an M1915 Adrian helmet featuring the infantry badge and an M1892 Lebel revolver, which he carries in a leather holster attached to an adjustable shoulder strap (*étui revolver M*1876/93). The ribbon on his chest is for the Croix de Guerre 1914–1918, awarded for acts of gallantry.

E2: *Chasseur*, 2ᵉ compagnie de skieurs, 21ᵉ bataillon mixte d'infanterie coloniale, Dvina River, December 1918

A French skier, around the start of the French Army's deployment in North Russia, with the distinctive headgear of the French Alpine troops, a sizeable beret (colloquially referred to as the *tarte* on account of its pie-like shape), made of dark blue-grey wool, to provide protection from the elements (this was routinely worn in combat, instead of the Adrian steel helmet). Also visible in this plate is part of the distinctive uniform of the *chasseurs alpins*, which consisted of a dark blue-grey *vareuse dolman* (tunic), matching trousers with a bright yellow-coloured pip along the outer seam, puttees, and hobnailed boots. His beret and tunic lapels (not visible here) feature the *brevet* (badge) of the *chasseurs alpins*, in the form of a stylized hunting horn, sewn in bright yellow (*jonquille jaune* or daffodil yellow) thread. His leather ammunition pouches, worn flanking the buckle of his two-prong M1903 leather belt, and supported by natural-leather Y-straps, are of the 1916 pattern. As a concession to the weather conditions (skiers did not normally wear greatcoats), he also wears the French Army's standard-issue, double-breasted, horizon-blue *capote* (greatcoat) with his hands tucked into its folded skirts.

E3: *Capitaine*, 1ᵉʳ compagnie, 16ᵉ régiment d'infanterie coloniale, Vladivostok, August 1918

A colonial infantry captain, at the time of the start of the deployment of the BCS to Siberia. He is turned out in tropical 'whites', and wears a privately-purchased pith helmet, similar to the Army-issue M1886 pith helmet. He is armed with a holstered M1892 Lebel revolver, and carries a leather map case. His tunic's gold domed buttons are adorned with the naval anchor, the symbol of France's colonial infantry.

F: CZECHOSLOVAK AND ITALIAN FORCES

F1: *Strelec*, 6th Rifle Regiment, Vladivostok, August 1920

The Czechoslovak Legionary portrayed here wears the new summer-issue brown-drab uniform introduced by virtue of Order No. 41 of 21 June 1919 (initially, only for officers). This included a stand-and-fall collar, straight-cuff tunic, fastening with five large plastic buttons and featuring four flap pockets (two on the breast and two on the skirts), and matching trousers, constrained by puttees. The bulk of the lower-ranking members of the Legion only received their new (so-called 'Vladivostok') uniforms shortly before their evacuation from Siberia. Officers sported Sam Browne-type waist belts, with their shoulder strap running over the right shoulder. The rifleman depicted here has four years of meritorious service with the Legion, indicated by the four inverted chevrons on his right upper sleeve. His decoration ribbons (only partly visible here) include, from left to right, the Czechoslovak Revolutionary Cross 1918–19, the Inter-Allied Victory Medal and the Czechoslovak War Cross 1918–19 (the highest Czechoslovak World War I bravery award). He is armed with an M1895 Mannlicher straight-pull bolt-action rifle, the principal Austro-Hungarian rifle of World War I.

F2: *Soldato*, IV Battaglione, 67° Reggimento di fanteria, Kola, November 1918

The Italian infantryman portrayed here, a member of the CSEO, wears the standard World War I period *grigio-verde* (grey-green) wool uniform, officially adopted on 4 December 1908 for all the branches of the Italian armed forces, except for the cavalry, to replace the Italian Army's dark-blue uniforms. His uniform consists of a five-button, fly-fronted, single-breasted *giubba* (tunic), with sewn-on epaulettes and a standing collar with brigade *mostrine* (patches) identifying his home unit, and comfortable trousers made of matching material, constrained by puttees. His headdress is the mod. 1916, a kepi-like, soft-crowned visored hat, displaying the regimental number in black thread. Adrian-type steel helmets (produced under French licence) were worn in combat; these displayed their wearer's unit number as well as the *freggio* corresponding to the branch of the armed forces to which he was assigned. For protection against the cold, he could wear the Italian Army's standard-issue greatcoat; a practical long *mantellina* (cape) was also issued to the troops. His belt equipment is of the grey-green pattern introduced in 1907, with four leather ammunition pouches for his 6.5mm M1891 Carcano bolt-action, internal box-fed rifle.

F3: *Strelec*, 1st (Jan Hus) Rifle Regiment, Penza, December 1918

The Czechoslovak rifleman portrayed here is turned out in an Imperial Russian Army double-breasted winter greatcoat (with oblong red collar patches); a Turkic *bashlik* hood, worn for protection against the intense cold; a pair of *valenki* heavy felt boots; and a typical Siberian fleece hat, which was 'hairier' compared to the standard *papakha*, adorned with a ribbon in white and red (the Czechoslovak colours). He is armed with a Russian Mosin-Nagant rifle, complete with its cruciform bayonet. Large numbers of Japanese Type 30 Arisaka rifles, some of them taken as war booty during the Russo-Japanese War, were also pressed into service to make up for the shortage of small arms that had plagued the Imperial Russian Army during World War I. Introduced into Japanese service in 1899, the Type 30 rifle had a hard-earned reputation for durability, ruggedness, accuracy and dependability.

G: WHITE RUSSIAN FORCES

G1: *Poruchik*, 1st Light Artillery Battery, Arkhangelsk, September 1918

This White Army field officer wears the summer version of the M1912 regulation uniform of the 'old' Russian Army, consisting of a superior quality, khaki *kittel* (tunic), dark-blue breeches (originally authorized for peacetime wear only) and riding boots. His headdress is the officers' *furashka*, complete with the Imperial Russian Army's oval-shaped cockade (for officers), while his shoulder boards identify him as an artillery officer (note the metal crossed-cannons insignia). His leather belt shoulder supports are worn vertically on his chest, distinguishing him from his contemporary Red Army commanders, who wore them criss-crossed, both on the chest and on the back. He carries the officers' version of the *shashka* sword (carried 'Oriental style' i.e., with its blade pointing forwards), and a binoculars case. The decoration of his chest is the Order of St Vladimir, 4th Class, with swords and bow, the second highest military decoration after the Order of St George.

G2: *Ryadovoy*, Izhevsk Rifle Brigade, Izhevsk People's Army, Transbaikalia, August 1919

An Izhevsk Rifle Regiment volunteer (formerly a metal worker), turned out in a mix of Allied clothing items, but with a peaked hat from former Imperial Russian Army stocks and Imperial Russian Army-styled white-over-blue shoulder boards on his tunic. His shoulder boards feature the 'Izh' cipher in Cyrillic script (for 'Izhevsk'), and their choice of colour is inspired by the iron and steel factories present in that part of Russia. His tunic and trousers are Imperial Russian Army-issue items, although by this stage in the Russian Civil War it was not infrequent for British and US Army tunics, trousers and boots to be worn by the anti-Bolshevik forces active throughout the territory of the former Russian Empire. He is armed with an M1891 Mosin-Nagant rifle.

G3: *Yefreytor*, 1st Northern Rifle Regiment, March 1919, Dvina River Front

Early in the intervention, the British supplied the Whites and the nationalist armies in the Baltics with stocks of surplus uniforms, boots and equipment, to replace depleted stocks of Imperial Russian Army items. This Northern Army NCO, inspired by a display at the Estonian War Museum (Tallinn), is turned out in a Pattern 1902 Service Dress tunic and trousers, a US Army M1917 double-breasted olive-drab overcoat, a pair of nondescript but foreign-supplied boots and a British steel Brodie helmet. Shoulder boards have been dropped, as a concession to the more republican elements of the Northern Army. He is armed with an M1891 Mosin-Nagant rifle.

H: BOLSHEVIK FORCES

H1: *Strelok*, 97th Saratov Regiment, Bolshoye Ozerki, April 1919

The surrendering rifleman portrayed here would have participated in the fighting at Bolshoye Ozerki, the last major engagement in North Russia, and a tactical victory for the Allies against the Red Army, in polar temperatures. He wears an M1910 *papakha* (winter cap) made of artificial astrakhan lambswool, an Imperial Russian Army-issue double-breasted greyish-brown M1911 greatcoat, 'old' Army regulation trousers constrained by puttees, and knee-length hobnailed leather boots. The cloth bandolier slung across his chest was designed to hold 30 rounds (in six clips) for his M1891 Mosin-Nagant (or three-line) rifle; although lightweight, these bandoliers were poorly designed, and the

Undated photograph showing a group of French Army officers, some in pith helmets, as they confer with some of their White Russian and Czechoslovak counterparts, most likely in Vladivostok, at the time of the arrival in Siberia of French colonial troops from Indochina in August 1918. (NARA)

clips they were supposed to hold often fell off. What distinguishes him as a Bolshevik is the diagonal red cloth ribbon on the front of his *papakha*, instead of the Imperial Russian cockade, the red cloth brassard on his left arm and the absence of shoulder boards from his greatcoat.

H2: Red Army commander, 18th Infantry Division, Tulgas, November 1918

A Red Army commander (or 'military specialist'), as he would have appeared during the Armistice Day Battle of Tulgas. To emphasize their authority, military commanders (the more neutral term used to describe the Red Army's holders of officer rank) but, also, commissars, often wore double-breasted leather jackets, which Trotsky considered as more than just an item of attire; these symbolized the new Red Army. In truth, leather jackets had previously been worn by the aviators and armoured vehicle drivers of the 'old' Army (but, also, by regular Army officers in the closing stages of World War I), and they were also favourites among political leaders, both during and after the Russian Civil War. The commander portrayed here is a bearer of the Order of the Banner, the Red Army's highest individual military award (established on 16 September 1918). He is armed with an M1895 Nagant revolver, tucked into his waist belt and secured by a lanyard, a common practice among Red Army troops pre-1922.

H3: Finnish Red Guard, Kandalakscha, October 1919

This plate, based on one of the displays at the Suomenlinna/ Sveaborg Museum (Helsinki), depicts a Finnish Red Guard at the time of the abortive attempt by 2/10th Royal Scots to capture the village of Kandalakscha, ending in a bloody ambush of the Allied troops, on 9 October 1919. Finnish Red Guards had established themselves in the Murmansk area after their defeat by the White Finns and had been, at one time, allies of the British in their struggle against the German forces, before turning against them. The Finnish partisan portrayed here wears civilian riding boots, a sheepskin-fur hat and civilian garb. He is armed with an M1891 Mosin-Nagant rifle and a Finnish hunting knife. White Russian reticence towards the White Finns' claims for independence deprived Finland's anti-Bolshevik movement of crucial support.

INDEX

Figures in **bold** refer to illustrations. Plates are shown with page and caption locators in parentheses.